MY KNITTED DOLL

MY KNITTED DOLL

Louise Crowther

DAVID & CHARLES

www.davidandcharles.com

CONTENTS

INTRODUCTION...8

TOOLS AND MATERIALS................................10

ABBREVIATIONS...13

Making the Dolls

Naomi..16

Grace..24

Ralph..32

Penny..38

Faye..44

Polly..52

Anna..58

Pippa..64

Jane..72

Alice..80

Florence..88

Martha..96

Techniques

Making up your doll...........................104

Casting on and stitches.....................110

Colourwork...118

Personalising your doll......................122

ABOUT THE AUTHOR...........................124

THANK YOU...124

SUPPLIERS..125

INDEX..126

INTRODUCTION

I'm delighted to introduce you to twelve adorable little people who are bound to make the little people in *your* life very happy indeed. I think we all had a doll or a teddy, or something similar, that we thought of as a best friend when we were growing up – someone to share adventures and make up stories with. The great thing about Penny, Grace, Anna, Ralph and the whole gang is that they are full of personality and have plenty of features like clothes, bags and hats that can enhance play and add to the fun. I've designed them all with play in mind, and given complete instructions to make knitting them a breeze.

The inspiration for my dolls comes mainly from all the beautiful children's clothes available on the high street, the gorgeous little dresses and trendy outfits I would love to buy and dress my little girl in... if only I'd had one!

I created my first doll back in 2010 after looking for a pattern to knit a gift for a friend's daughter. There is something very special and satisfying about seeing a child all snuggled up with a toy that you have lovingly made. I wanted something different, something other than the traditional knitted dolls I remembered from my childhood, something

that was stylish and cute rather than brash and garish. Unable to find anything suitable I decided to have a go at making my own pattern, with the contemporary look I had in mind. The resulting doll was a resounding success and I soon became inundated with requests for more dolls.

Each pattern is written in a straight forward, easy-to-follow manner with row by row instructions, so that even the less-experienced knitter will find them easy to follow. The patterns in this book are designed for you and your friends and family to enjoy and for private use only.

Finally, please look at the section on personalising your knitted doll. You can treat any of the dolls as a starting point and adapt the hair, clothing, colours and features to make the perfect doll for you. I look forward to seeing photos of your knitted dolls, share them using the hashtag #myknitteddoll and you can see everyone else's too.

Hope you enjoy knitting these dolls as much as I have enjoyed creating them,

xo *Louise*

TOOLS & MATERIALS

There are so many yarns and needles, and other bits and bobs available in specialist stores and online that I thought I should give you a brief guide to the things I use to achieve the look of the dolls you can see in this book.

YARN

The dolls in this book have all been made using 4 ply (fingering) weight yarn in 100% cotton. I love the crisp, clean look of 100% cotton yarn. It is non-allergic for most people, incredibly robust and stands up well to being played with.

Various brands of cotton yarn have been used for these dolls, mainly Patons 100% cotton 4 ply, Puppets Lyric 4 ply, Anchor Creativa Fino Cotton and Scheepjes Catona (please refer to Suppliers at the back of the book).

Although I recommend using 100% cotton yarn to achieve the same look and feel as my dolls, the patterns will work just as well with any 4 ply non-fancy spun yarn.

Tip

BECAUSE THE DOLLS ARE RELATIVELY SMALL YOU WILL ONLY NEED A SMALL AMOUNT OF EACH COLOUR OF YARN – A 25G BALL OF YARN IN EACH WOULD EASILY BE ENOUGH.

NEEDLES

You will need a pair of each of 2.5mm and 3mm straight needles and two 2.5mm double pointed needles to complete each doll.

You may need to adjust your needle sizes to accommodate your own personal tension, I am quite a tight knitter but many of you may knit loosely and therefore will need to adjust your needle size to achieve the correct gauge.

All the dolls in this book should have the same gauge: 35 sts and 48 rows to 10cm (4in) in stocking stitch on 2.5mm needles.

STUFFING

I recommend a synthetic high-loft polyester toy filling for stuffing these dolls. It is lovely and soft, holds its shape well and is hand or machine washable on a cool delicate cycle.

When stuffing your doll use small pieces, roll and manipulate the body parts in your hands to spread the stuffing evenly and ensure a smooth shape. Tease out any lumps using a blunt tapestry needle carefully inserted through the knitting in the gap between stitches.

YOU WILL ALSO NEED

White felt

Small circles of white felt (roughly 15mm (½in) diameter) are used to strengthen the knitted fabric behind the facial features and prevent the knotted ends showing through to the right side.

Basic kit and embellishments

The other items you need to complete each doll are listed at the beginning of each project. The following is a basic guide:

· Tapestry needle

· Stitch holder

· Stitch markers

· Small buttons, 6mm (¼in) diameter

· Sewing needle and thread

· Ribbon, small lengths 5mm (³⁄₁₆in) wide

· Scissors

WASHING

If made in 100% cotton yarn and stuffed with synthetic toy filling, these dolls can either be washed by hand or on a gentle cool machine cycle. I would recommend reshaping the dolls and their clothing whilst still damp.

Safety note

DO NOT USE SAFETY EYES, BUTTONS, BEADS OR GLASS EYES ON TOYS INTENDED FOR CHILDREN UNDER THREE YEARS OLD AS THEY ARE A POTENTIAL CHOKING HAZARD.

ABBREVIATIONS

dpn	Double pointed needle	pm	Place marker
K	Knit	PSSO	Pass slipped stitch/stitches over
K2tog	Knit two stitches together		
K3tog	Knit three stitches together	pw	Purlwise
Kfb	Knit one stitch through front loop, then knit through back loop	rpt	Repeat
		sl1	Slip one stitch
		sl2tog	Slip two stitches together
Ktbl	Knit stitch through back loop	sm	Slip marker
		SSK	Slip two stitches knitwise one at a time, knit together through back loops
kw	Knitwise		
M1	Make one stitch: from the front, lift loop between stitches with left needle, knit into back of loop		
		SSP	Slip two stitches knitwise one at a time, purl together through back loops
m1l	Make one left: from the front, lift loop between stitches with left needle, knit into back of loop		
		SSSK	Slip 3 stitches knitwise one at a time, knit together through back loops
m1r	Make one right: from the back, lift loop between stitches with left needle, knit into front of loop	St(s)	Stitch(es)
		Stocking Stitch	Knit all stitches on right side rows, purl all stitches on wrong side rows
P	Purl	ws	Wrong Side
P2tog	Purl two stitches together	wyif	With yarn in front
Pfb	Purl one stitch through front loop, then purl through back loop	YO	Yarn over

MAKING
THE DOLLS

Naomi

She's reached the sweet shop, but Naomi's sure she's forgotten something. Whatever it is, perhaps it's in her little flower bag, or maybe she dropped it when she was admiring the fact that the paper bags are striped like her tights? Naomi's a bit of a daydreamer. She wears her bobble hat all year round, otherwise she might lose that too.

You Will Need

Yarn

- **Yarn A** Beige
- **Yarn B** Pale Yellow
- **Yarn C** Navy
- **Yarn D** Pink
- **Yarn E** Cerise
- **Yarn F** Cream
- **Yarn G** Moss Green
- **Yarn H** Burgundy
- Scraps of black and red for eyes and mouth

You will also need

- 3mm (US 2½) straight needles
- 2.5mm (US 1½) straight needles
- 2.5mm (US 1½) double-pointed needles
- Stitch holder
- Tapestry needle
- 3 x 15mm (½in) circles of white felt
- Toy stuffing
- 5 x 6mm (¼in) buttons
- 1 x 6.5cm (2½in) long piece of card

Finished size

- 28cm (11in) tall

Pattern

Cast on using the Long-tail (double cast on) method (see Techniques) unless otherwise indicated. Where possible leave long tails when you cast on and cast off and use these for the sewing up.

Head

Using Yarn A and 2.5mm needles cast on 13 sts.

Starting at neck:

Row 1 (ws): Purl.

Row 2: [K1, M1] 12 times, K1. (25 sts)

Row 3: Purl.

Row 4: K3, [K1, M1] 7 times, K4, [K1, M1] 7 times, K4. (39 sts)

Rows 5–7: Stocking stitch 3 rows.

Row 8: K3, [K3, M1] 4 times, K6, [K3, M1] 4 times, K6. (47 sts)

Cut yarn

Rows 9–31: Using intarsia technique (see Techniques) and working in stocking stitch work hair chart. Start with a purl row (ws) at the bottom left hand corner of chart, read purl rows (ws) from left to right and knit rows (rs) from right to left.

For top of head continue in Yarn B.

Row 32: K8, K2tog, K4, SSK, K15, K2tog, K4, SSK, K8. (43 sts)

Row 33: Purl.

Row 34: K8, K2tog, K2, SSK, K15, K2tog, K2, SSK, K8. (39 sts)

Row 35: Purl.

Row 36: K8, K2tog, SSK, K15, K2tog, SSK, K8. (35 sts)

Cut yarn, transfer the stitches on to a stitch holder.

Body

T-SHIRT

Using Yarn D and 2.5mm needles cast on 9 sts.

Starting at neck:

Row 1 (ws): Purl.

Row 2: K1, [K1, M1] 6 times, K2. (15 sts)

Row 3: Purl.

Row 4: K2, [K1, M1] 3 times, K4, [K1, M1] 3 times, K3. (21 sts)

Row 5: Purl.

Row 6: K3, [K1, M1] 4 times, K6, [K1, M1] 4 times, K4. (29 sts)

Rows 7–9: Stocking stitch 3 rows.

Row 10: K4, [K1, M1] 6 times, K8, [K1, M1] 6 times, K5. (41 sts)

Rows 11–15: Stocking stitch 5 rows.

Row 16: K3, [K3, M1] 4 times, K8, [K3, M1] 4 times, K6. (49 sts)

Rows 17–25: Stocking stitch 9 rows.

Rows 26–27: Knit 2 rows.

TOP OF TIGHTS

Continue working the 49 sts on needle.

Change to Yarn F.

Rows 28–29: Starting with a knit row, stocking stitch 2 rows.

Change to Yarn D.

Rows 30–33: Stocking stitch 4 rows.

Change to Yarn F.

Rows 34–35: Stocking stitch 2 rows.

Change to Yarn D.

Rows 36–37: Stocking stitch 2 rows.

Change to Yarn F.

Rows 38–39: Stocking stitch 2 rows.

Change to Yarn D.

Rows 40–43: Stocking stitch 4 rows.

Cast off.

Arms

(make 2)

Using Yarn A and 2.5mm needles cast on 12 sts.

Rows 1–3: Starting with a purl row (ws), stocking stitch 3 rows.

Row 4: Cast on 3 sts using knit cast on method (see Techniques), knit to end. (15 sts)

Row 5: Cast on 3 sts using purl cast-on method (see Techniques section), purl to end. (18 sts)

Rows 6–7: Stocking stitch 2 rows.

Row 8: SSK, K14, K2tog. (16 sts)

Row 9: Purl.

Row 10: SSK, K12, K2tog. (14 sts)

Row 11: Purl.

Row 12: SSK, K10, K2tog. (12 sts)

Rows 13–31: Stocking stitch 19 rows.

Change to Yarn D.

Rows 32–33: Knit 2 rows.

Rows 34–47: Starting with a knit row, stocking stitch 14 rows.

Row 48: SSK, K8, K2tog. (10 sts)

Row 49: Purl.

Row 50: SSK, K6, K2tog. (8 sts)

Row 51: Purl.

Row 52: SSK, K4, K2tog. (6 sts)

Row 53: Purl.

Row 54: SSK, K2, K2tog. (4 sts)

Row 55: Purl.

Cast off.

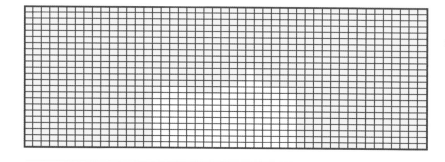

Hair Chart

□ = Yarn A   □ = Yarn B

Legs

(make 2)

Starting at top of leg:

Using Yarn F and 2.5mm needles cast on 16 sts.

Row 1 (ws): Purl.

Change to Yarn D.

Rows 2–3: Stocking stitch 2 rows.

Change to Yarn F.

Rows 4–5: Stocking stitch 2 rows.

Change to Yarn D.

Rows 6–9: Stocking stitch 4 rows.

Change to Yarn F.

Rows 10–11: Stocking stitch 2 rows.

Continue in stripe pattern of 2 rows Yarn D, 2 rows Yarn F, 4 rows Yarn D and 2 rows Yarn F throughout leg.

Rows 12–55: Stocking stitch 44 rows.

TOP OF FOOT

Row 56: Cast off 5 sts, knit to end. (11 sts)

Row 57: Cast off 5 sts pw, purl to end. (6 sts)

Rows 58–75: Stocking stitch 18 rows.

Cast off row: SSK, K2, K2tog (cast off all sts as you work them).

Mary Jane shoes

(make 2)

Using Yarn C and 2.5mm needles cast on 12 sts.

Row 1 (ws): Purl.

Row 2: K1, M1, K3, [K1, M1] 3 times, K4, M1, K1. (17 sts)

Row 3: Purl.

Row 4: [K1, M1] 2 times, K3, [K1, M1] 2 times, K2, [K1, M1] 2 times, K3, [K1, M1] 2 times, K1. (25 sts)

Row 5: Purl.

Row 6: [K2, M1] 2 times, K2, [K2, M1] 2 times, K3, [K2, M1] 2 times, K2, [K2, M1] 2 times, K2. (33 sts)

Row 7: Purl.

Row 8: [K3, M1] 2 times, K1, [K3, M1] 2 times, K4, [K3, M1] 2 times, K1, [K3, M1] 2 times, K3. (41 sts)

Rows 9–13: Stocking stitch 5 rows.

Row 14: K15, SSK, K7, K2tog, K15. (39 sts)

Row 15: Purl.

Row 16: K15, SSK, K5, K2tog, K15. (37 sts)

Row 17: Purl.

Cast off row: K15, SSK, K3, K2tog, K15 (cast off all sts as you work them).

Shoe straps

(make 2)

Using Yarn C and 2.5mm needles cast on 10 sts.

Row 1 (ws): K7, P3.

Row 2: K3, turn.

Row 3: P3.

Cast off knitwise.

Dress

Front of dress

Using Yarn C and 3mm needles cast on 37 sts.

Row 1 (ws): Knit.

Row 2: Knit.

Row 3: Purl.

Rows 4–5: Knit 2 rows.

Rows 6–7: Starting with a knit row, stocking stitch 2 rows.

Rows 8–20: Using Fair Isle (stranded) technique (see Techniques) and working in stocking stitch, work Dress Chart across the stitches, start with a knit row (rs) at the bottom right-hand corner of the chart. Read knit rows (rs) from right to left and purl rows (ws) from left to right.

Rows 21–37: Stocking stitch 17 rows.

Row 38: [K1, K2tog] to last st, K1. (25 sts)

Row 39: Purl.

Row 40: K1, SSK, K19, K2tog, K1. (23 sts)

Row 41: Purl.

Row 42: K1, SSK, K17, K2tog, K1. (21 sts)

Row 43: Purl.

Row 44: K1, SSK, K15, K2tog, K1. (19 sts)

Rows 45–53: Stocking stitch 9 rows.

Cast off.

Dress Chart

■ = Yarn C
□ = Yarn D
■ = Yarn E
□ = Yarn F
■ = Yarn G
■ = Yarn H

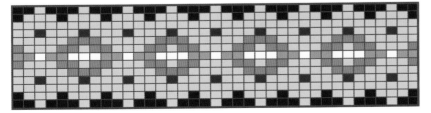

Back of dress

Using Yarn C and 3mm needles cast on 37 sts.

Row 1 (ws): Knit.

Row 2: Knit.

Row 3: Purl.

Rows 4–5: Knit 2 rows.

Row 6–7: Starting with a knit row, stocking stitch 2 rows.

Rows 8–20: Work Dress Chart (see Front of Dress).

Rows 21–37: Stocking stitch 17 rows.

Row 38: [K1, K2tog] to last st, K1. (25 sts)

Row 39: Purl.

RIGHT BUTTON PLACKET

Row 40: K1, SSK, K11, turn. (13 sts)

Row 41: K3, P10.

Row 42: K1, SSK, K10, turn. (12 sts)

Row 43: K3, P9.

Row 44: K1, SSK, K7, YO, K2tog, turn. (11 sts)

Row 45: K1, Ktbl, K1, P8.

Row 46: K11, turn.

Row 47: K3, P8.

Rows 48–51: Rpt last 2 rows, 2 more times.

Row 52: K9, YO, K2tog, turn.

Row 53: K1, Ktbl, K1, P8.

Cast off 11 sts, cut yarn.

LEFT BUTTON PLACKET

Row 1: Returning to stitches still on needle, rejoin Yarn C and pick up and knit 3 sts from behind the first row of right button placket (see Techniques, Picking Up Stitches), knit across stitches on left-hand needle to last 3 sts, K2tog, K1. (13 sts)

Row 2: P10, K3.

Row 3: Knit to last 3 sts, K2tog, K1. (12 sts)

Row 4: P9, K3.

Row 5: Knit to last 3 sts, K2tog, K1. (11 sts)

Row 6: P8, K3.

Row 7: Knit.

Rows 8–13: Rpt last 2 rows, 3 more times.

Row 14: P8, K3.

Cast off.

Bolero jacket

Bolero front right side

Using Yarn E and 3mm needles cast on 6 sts.

Row 1 (ws): Knit.

Row 2: K2, Kfb, K3. (7 sts)

Row 3: P4, Pfb, K2. (8 sts)

Row 4: K2, Kfb, K5. (9 sts)

Row 5: P7, K2.

Row 6: K2, Kfb, K6. (10 sts)

Row 7: P8, K2.

Row 8: K2, Kfb, K7. (11 sts)

Row 9: P9, K2.

Row 10: Knit.

Rows 11–14: Rpt last 2 rows, 2 more times.

Row 15: P9, K2.

Row 16: K2, SSK, K7. (10 sts)

Row 17: P8, K2.

Row 18: K2, SSK, K6. (9 sts)

Row 19: P7, K2.

Row 20: K2, SSK, K5. (8 sts)

Row 21: P4, SSP, K2. (7 sts)

Row 22: K2, SSK, K3. (6 sts)

Row 23: P4, K2.

Cast off.

Bolero front left side

Using Yarn E and 3mm needles cast on 6 sts.

Row 1 (ws): Knit.

Row 2: K2, Kfb, K3. (7 sts)

Row 3: K2, P1, Pfb, P3. (8sts)

Row 4: K4, Kfb, K3. (9 sts)

Row 5: K2, P7.

Row 6: K5, Kfb, K3. (10 sts)

Row 7: K2, P8.

Row 8: K6, Kfb, K3. (11 sts)

Row 9: K2, P9.

Row 10: Knit.

Rows 11–14: Rpt last 2 rows, 2 more times.

Row 15: K2, P9.

Row 16: K7, K2tog, K2. (10 sts)

Row 17: K2, P8.

Row 18: K6, K2tog, K2. (9 sts)

Row 19: K2, P7.

Row 20: K5, K2tog, K2. (8 sts)

Row 21: K2, P2tog, P4. (7 sts)

Row 22: K3, K2tog, K2. (6 sts)

Row 23: K2, P4.

Cast off.

Bolero back

Using Yarn E and 3mm needles cast on 25 sts.

Row 1 (ws): Knit.

Rows 2–23: Starting with a knit row, stocking stitch 22 rows.

Cast off.

Sleeves

(make 2)

Using Yarn E and 3mm needles cast on 14 sts.

Row 1 (ws): Knit.

Row 2: [K1, Kfb] to last 2 sts, K2. (20 sts)

Rows 3–21: Stocking stitch 19 rows.

Cast off.

Bobble hat

Using Yarn C and 2.5mm needles cast on 51 sts.

Row 1 (ws): P1, [K1, P2] to last 2 sts, K1, P1.

Row 2: K1, [P1, K2] to last 2 sts, P1, K1.

Rows 3–16: Rpt last 2 rows 7 more times.

Row 17: P1, [K1, P2] to last 2 sts, K1, P1.

Row 18: K1, P1, [K2tog, P1] to last st, K1. (35 sts)

Row 19: [P1, K1] to last st, P1.

Row 20: [K1, P1] to last st, K1.

Rows 21–22: Rpt last 2 rows.

Row 23: [P1, K1] to last st, P1.

Row 24: K1, [K2tog] to end (18 sts)

Rows 25–27: Starting with a purl row, stocking stitch 3 rows.

Row 28: K1, [K2tog] to last st, K1. (10 sts)

Cut yarn leaving a long tail. Using a tapestry needle thread tail through the stitches left on needle and draw up.

Bobble

Using Yarn D and 3mm needles cast on 4 sts.

Row 1 (ws): Pfb, P2, Pfb. (6 sts)

Rows 2–5: Starting with a knit row, stocking stitch 4 rows.

Row 6: SSK, K2, K2tog. (4 sts)

Row 7: P2tog, P2tog, pass 1st stitch over last, cut yarn leaving a long tail and pull through remaining stitch. Using the yarn tail sew a running stitch around the outer edge of bobble and pull tightly. Knot both tail ends together to secure.

Flower bag

Using Yarn G and 3mm needles cast on 24 sts.

Row 1 (ws): Purl.

Row 2: [K1, M1] 2 times, K7, [K1, M1] 2 times, K1, [K1, M1] 2 times, K7, [K1, M1] 2 times, K1. (32 sts)

Rows 3–4: Knit 2 rows.

Row 5: [P2, K1] to last 2 sts, P2.

Rows 6–8: Knit 3 rows.

Rows 9–16: Rep rows 5–8, 2 more times.

Row 17: Rep row 5.

Rows 18–19: Knit 2 rows.

Row 20: K5, cast off 6 sts, K10, cast off 6 sts, Knit to end. (20 sts)

Row 21: K4, *Kfb, pass knitted front-loop stitch over knitted back-loop stitch and pull yarn tight, turn, cast on 13 sts, turn, slip last cast on stitch onto left needle, K2tog and pull yarn tight*, K8; rpt from * to *, K4.

Cast off knitwise.

Flower

Using Yarn D and 2.5mm needles cast on 31 sts.

FIRST PETAL

Row 1 (ws): Slip 1 purlwise, P5, turn.

Row 2: K5, turn.

Row 3: P5, turn.

Row 4: K6, turn.

Row 5: [P2tog] 3 times.

REMAINING PETALS

Rpt rows 1–5, 4 more times until 1 st remains, P1.

Next row: K1, [slip 2 together knitwise, K1, PSSO] to end.

Cut yarn leaving a long tail. Using a tapestry needle thread the tail through the stitches left on needle and draw up.

Making Up

Doll

See Making Up Your Doll in Techniques.

Plaits

(make 2)

1. See Making Plaits in Techniques.
2. Sew the plaits in place on either side of the completed head **(A)**.

Clothing & accessories

Bolero jacket

1. Block all the pieces of the bolero before making up.
2. Start by sewing up the shoulder seams, then sew the arms to the front and back pieces, lining up the centre of the arms to the shoulder seams.
3. Sew up the arm and body edge seams to finish.

DRESS

1. Block all the pieces of the dress before making up.
2. Start by sewing the buttons into place on the back of the dress, matching them up with the button holes **(B)**.
3. Sew up the shoulder seams making sure you leave a big enough gap to fit around Naomi's neck.
4. Matching up the Fair Isle pattern sew up the edge seams, leaving a 2½cm (1in) gap at the top for the arm holes.

Bobble hat

1. Block the hat before you begin.
2. Sew the side edges together.
3. Stitch the bobble in place on the top of the hat.

Flower bag

1. Block bag piece before you make up.
2. Start by sewing the side and bottom edges together.
3. Join the first and last petals of the flower together at the 'cast on' edge with a small stitch.
4. Sew onto the front of the bag then add a contrasting button in the centre of the flower to finish.

Grace

Some people wear their heart on their sleeve, but Grace prefers to wear hers on her pinafore. Friendship bracelets, hair bobbles, and making slightly lop-sided gifts for granny are just a few of her favourite things. Being a caring crusader means getting through a lot of beads, glitter and sparkly stickers, but it's worth it to make people smile.

You Will Need

Yarn

Yarn A Beige

Yarn B Orange

Yarn C Aqua

Yarn D Turquoise

Yarn E Bright Red

Yarn F Cream

Scraps of black and red for eyes and mouth

Finished size

28cm (11in) tall

You will also need

3mm (US 2½) straight needles

2.5mm (US ½) straight needles

2.5mm (US ½) double-pointed needles

Stitch holder

Tapestry needle

3 x 15mm (½in) circles of white felt

Toy stuffing

5 x 6mm (¼in) buttons

Pattern

Cast on using the Long-tail (double cast on) method (see Techniques) unless otherwise indicated. Where possible leave long tails when you cast on and cast off and use these for the sewing up.

Head

Starting at neck:

Using Yarn A and 2.5mm needles cast on 13 sts.

Row 1 (ws): Purl.

Row 2: [K1, M1] 12 times, K1. (25 sts)

Row 3: Purl.

Row 4: K3, [K1, M1] 7 times, K4, [K1, M1] 7 times, K4. (39 sts)

Rows 5–7: Stocking stitch 3 rows.

Row 8: K3, [K3, M1] 4 times, K6, [K3, M1] 4 times, K6. (47 sts)

Cut yarn.

Rows 9–31: Using intarsia technique (see Techniques) and working in stocking stitch work Hair Chart. Start with a purl row (ws) at the bottom left hand corner of chart, read purl rows (ws) from left to right and knit rows (rs) from right to left.

For top of head continue in Yarn B.

Row 32: K8, K2tog, K4, SSK, K15, K2tog, K4, SSK, K8. (43 sts)

Row 33: Purl.

Row 34: K8, K2tog, K2, SSK, K15, K2tog, K2, SSK, K8. (39 sts)

Row 35: Purl.

Row 36: K8, K2tog, SSK, K15, K2tog, SSK, K8. (35 sts)

Cut yarn, transfer the stitches onto a stitch holder.

Pigtails

(make 2)

Using Yarn B and 2.5mm needles cast on 10 sts.

Row 1 (ws): Purl.

Row 2: K4, M1, [K1, M1] 2 times, K4. (13 sts)

Row 3: Purl.

Row 4: K6, M1, K1, M1, K6. (15 sts)

Row 5: Purl

Row 6: K7, M1, K1, M1, K7. (17 sts)

Row 7: Purl.

Row 8: SSK, K13, K2tog. (15 sts)

Row 9: Purl.

Row 10: K5, cast off 5 sts, K to end. (10 sts)

Row 11: P4, P2tog, P4. (9 sts)

Row 12: SSK, K5, K2tog. (7 sts)

Rows 13–15: Stocking stitch 3 rows.

Row 16: K1, SSK, K1, K2tog, K1. (5 sts)

Row 17: Purl.

Cut yarn leaving a long tail, thread tail through the stitches left on needle and draw up.

Hair scrunchies

(make 2)

Using 2.5mm double pointed needles and Yarn D, cast on 3 sts and make an i-cord of 8 rows (see Techniques).

Body

Using Yarn A and 2.5mm needles cast on 9 sts.

Starting at neck:

Row 1 (ws): Purl.

Row 2: K1, [K1, M1] 6 times, K2. (15 sts)

Row 3: Purl.

Row 4: K2, [K1, M1] 3 times, K4, [K1, M1] 3 times, K3. (21 sts)

Row 5: Purl.

Row 6: K3, [K1, M1] 4 times, K6, [K1, M1] 4 times, K4. (29 sts)

Rows 7–9: Stocking stitch 3 rows.

Row 10: K4, [K1, M1] 6 times, K8, [K1, M1] 6 times, K5. (41 sts)

Rows 11–15: Stocking stitch 5 rows.

Row 16: K3, [K3, M1] 4 times, K8, [K3, M1] 4 times, K6. (49 sts)

Rows 17–27: Stocking stitch 11 rows.

TOP OF TIGHTS

Continue working the 49 sts on needle.

Starting with Yarn C, the tights are worked in a stripe pattern of 2 rows Yarn C and 2 rows Yarn F throughout.

Rows 28–29: Knit 2 rows.

Rows 30–43: Starting with a knit row, stocking stitch 14 rows.

Cast off using Yarn C.

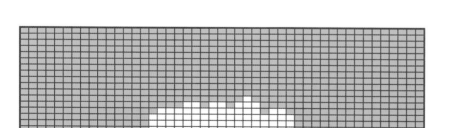

Hair Chart

□ = Yarn A
▨ = Yarn B

Arms

Left arm

Using Yarn A and 2.5mm needles cast on 12 sts.

Rows 1–3: Starting with a purl row (ws), stocking stitch 3 rows.

Row 4: Cast on 3 sts using Knit Cast-on method (see Techniques), knit to end. (15 sts)

Row 5: Cast on 3 sts using Purl Cast-on method (see Techniques), purl to end. (18 sts)

Rows 6–7: Stocking stitch 2 rows.

Row 8: SSK, K14, K2tog. (16 sts)

Row 9: Purl.

Row 10: SSK, K12, K2tog. (14 sts)

Row 11: Purl.

Row 12: SSK, K10, K2tog. (12 sts)

Row 13: Purl.

BRACELET

The next 4 rows form the bracelet.

Change to Yarn E.

Row 14: Knit.

Change to 3mm needles for next 2 rows.

Row 15: Purl

Row 16: K1, [YO, K2tog] to last st, K1.

Change to 2.5mm needles.

Row 17: Purl.

Change to Yarn A.

Rows 18–47: Stocking stitch 30 rows.

Row 48: SSK, K8, K2tog. (10 sts)

Row 49: Purl.

Row 50: SSK, K6, K2tog. (8 sts)

Row 51: Purl.

Row 52: SSK, K4, K2tog. (6 sts)

Row 53: Purl.

Row 54: SSK, K2, K2tog. (4sts)

Row 55: Purl.

Cast off.

Right arm

Rows 1–12: Work as Left Arm rows 1–12.

Rows 13–47: Stocking stitch 35 rows.

Row 48: SSK, K8, K2tog. (10 sts)

Row 49: Purl.

Row 50: SSK, K6, K2tog. (8 sts)

Row 51: Purl.

Row 52: SSK, K4, K2tog. (6 sts)

Row 53: Purl.

Row 54: SSK, K2, K2tog. (4 sts)

Row 55: Purl.

Cast off.

Legs

(make 2)

Starting at top of leg:

Using Yarn C and 2.5mm needles cast on 16 sts.

Row 1 (ws): Purl.

From this point onwards the legs are worked in a stripe pattern of 2 rows Yarn F and 2 rows Yarn C, starting with Yarn F.

Rows 2–55: Continue in stocking stitch for a further 54 rows.

TOP OF FOOT

Row 56: Cast off 5 sts, knit to end. (11 sts)

Row 57: Cast off 5 sts pw, purl to end. (6 sts)

Rows 58–75: Stocking stitch 18 rows.

Cast off row: SSK, K2, K2tog (cast off all sts as you work them).

T-bar shoes

(make 2)

Using Yarn E and 2.5mm needles cast on 12 sts.

Row 1 (ws): Purl.

Row 2: K1, M1, K3, [K1, M1] 3 times, K4, M1, K1. (17 sts)

Row 3: Purl.

Row 4: [K1, M1] 2 times, K3, [K1, M1] 2 times, K2, [K1, M1] 2 times, K3, [K1, M1] 2 times, K1. (25 sts)

Row 5: Purl.

Row 6: [K2, M1] 2 times, K2, [K2, M1] 2 times, K3, [K2, M1] 2 times, K2, [K2, M1] 2 times, K2. (33 sts)

Row 7: Purl.

Row 8: [K3, M1] 2 times, K1, [K3, M1] 2 times, K4, [K3, M1] 2 times, K1, [K3, M1] 2 times, K3. (41 sts)

Rows 9–13: Stocking stitch 5 rows.

Row 14: K15, SSK, K7, K2tog, K15. (39 sts)

Row 15: Purl.

Row 16: K15, SSK, K5, K2tog, K15. (37 sts)

Row 17: Purl.

Row 18: Cast off 15 sts, SSK, K3, k2tog, knit to end. (20 sts)

Row 19: Cast off 15 sts pw, purl to end. (5 sts)

Row 20: SSK, K1, K2tog.

Row 21: K1, P1, K1.

Row 22: Knit.

Rows 23–29: Rpt last 2 rows, 3 more times, then rpt row 21 once more.

Row 30: K1, sl1 pw with yarn at back, K1.

Row 31: K1, sl1 pw with yarn at front, K1. Cast off.

Shoe straps

(make 2)

Using Yarn E and 2.5mm needles cast on 10 sts.

Row 1 (ws): K7, P3.

Row 2: K3, turn.

Row 3: P3.

Cast off knitwise.

Dress

Front of dress

Using Yarn D and 2.5mm needles cast on 35 sts.

Rows 1–3: Starting with a purl row (ws), stocking stitch 3 rows.

Row 4: K1, [YO, K2tog] to end (35 sts)

Change to 3mm needles

Rows 5–9: Stocking stitch 5 rows.

The next 36 rows are worked in a stripe pattern of 6 rows Yarn C and 6 rows Yarn D, starting with Yarn C.

Rows 10–12: Stocking stitch 3 rows.

The Dress Chart is placed in the following rows using Intarsia technique (see Techniques) and worked in stocking stitch. Starting at the bottom left corner, read purl (ws) rows from left to right and knit (rs) rows from right to left.

Row 13: P16, work Dress Chart, P4.

Row 14: K4, work Dress Chart, K16.

Row 15–28: Repeat the last 2 rows 7 more times.

Rows 29–43: Continue in stocking stitch for a further 15 rows.

Row 44: [K2tog, K1] to last 2 sts, K2tog. (23 sts)

Row 45: Purl.

Change to Yarn C.

Row 46: K1, SSK, K17, K2tog, K1. (21 sts)

Row 47: Purl.

Row 48: K1, SSK, K15, K2tog, K1. (19 sts)

Row 49: Purl.

Row 50: K1, SSK, K13, K2tog, K1. (17 sts)

Rows 51–59: Stocking stitch 9 rows. Cast off.

Back of dress

Using Yarn D and 2.5mm needles cast on 35 sts.

Rows 1–3: Starting with a purl row (ws), stocking stitch 3 rows.

Row 4: K1, [YO, K2tog] to end. (35 sts).

Change to 3mm needles.

Rows 5–9: Stocking stitch 5 rows.

The next 36 rows are worked in a stripe pattern of 6 rows Yarn C and 6 rows Yarn D, starting with Yarn C.

Rows 10–43: Continue in stocking stitch for a further 34 rows.

Row 44: [K2tog, K1] to last 2 sts, K2tog. (23 sts)

Row 45: Purl.

RIGHT BUTTON PLACKET

Change to Yarn C.

Row 46: K1, SSK, K10, turn. (12 sts)

Row 47: K3, P9.

Row 48: K1, SSK, K9, turn. (11 sts)

Row 49: K3, P8.

Row 50: K1, SSK, K6, YO, K2tog, turn. (10 sts)

Row 51: K1, Ktbl, K1, P7.

Row 52: K10, turn.

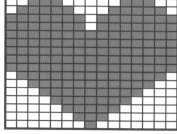

Dress Chart

□ = Yarn C/D (stripe pattern)

■ = Yarn E

Row 53: K3, P7.

Rows 54–57: Rpt last 2 rows, 2 more times.

Row 58: K8, YO, K2tog, turn.

Row 59: K1, Ktbl, K1, P7.

Cast off 10 sts, cut yarn.

LEFT BUTTON PLACKET

Row 1: Returning to stitches still on needle, rejoin Yarn C and pick up and knit 3 sts from BEHIND the first row of Right Button Placket (see Techniques, Picking up Stitches), knit across stitches on left hand needle to last 3 sts, K2tog, K1. (12 sts)

Row 2: P9, K3.

Row 3: K9, K2tog, K1. (11 sts)

Row 4: P8, K3.

Row 5: K8, K2tog, K1. (10 sts)

Row 6: P7, K3.

Row 7: Knit.

Rows 8–13: Rpt last 2 rows, 3 more times.

Row 14: P7, K3.

Cast off.

Shrug

Right front of shrug

Using Yarn F and 3mm needles cast on 6 sts.

Row 1 (ws): Knit.

Row 2: K2, Kfb, K3. (7 sts)

Row 3: P4, Pfb, K2. (8 sts)

Row 4: K2, Kfb, K5. (9 sts)

Row 5: P7, K2.

Row 6: K2, Kfb, K6. (10 sts)

Row 7: P8, K2.

Row 8: K2, Kfb, K7. (11 sts)

Row 9: P9, K2.

Row 10: Knit.

Rows 11–14: Rpt last 2 rows, 2 more times.

Row 15: P9, K2.

Row 16: K2, SSK, K7. (10 sts)

Row 17: P8, K2.

Row 18: K2, SSK, K6. (9 sts)

Row 19: P7, K2.

Row 20: K2, SSK, K5. (8 sts)

Row 21: P4, SSP, K2. (7 sts)

Row 22: K2, SSK, K3. (6 sts)

Row 23: P4, K2.

Cast off.

Left front of shrug

Using Yarn F and 3mm needles cast on 6 sts.

Row 1 (ws): Knit.

Row 2: K2, Kfb, K3. (7 sts)

Row 3: K2, P1, Pfb, P3. (8sts)

Row 4: K4, Kfb, K3. (9 sts)

Row 5: K2, P7.

Row 6: K5, Kfb, K3. (10 sts)

Row 7: K2, P8.

Row 8: K6, Kfb, K3. (11 sts)

Row 9: K2, P9.

Row 10: Knit.

Rows 11–14: Rpt last 2 rows, 2 more times.

Row 15: K2, P9.

Row 16: K7, K2tog, K2. (10 sts)

Row 17: K2, P8.

Row 18: K6, K2tog, K2. (9 sts)

Row 19: K2, P7.

Row 20: K5, K2tog, K2. (8 sts)

Row 21: K2, P2tog, P4. (7 sts)

Row 22: K3, K2tog, K2. (6 sts)

Row 23: K2, P4.

Cast off.

Back of shrug

Using Yarn F and 3mm needles cast on 25 sts.

Row 1 (ws): Knit

Rows 2–23: Starting with a knit row, stocking stitch 22 rows.

Cast off

Sleeves

(make 2)

Using Yarn F and 3mm needles cast on 20 sts.

Row 1 (ws): Knit

Rows 2–11: Starting with a knit row, stocking stitch 10 rows.

Cast off.

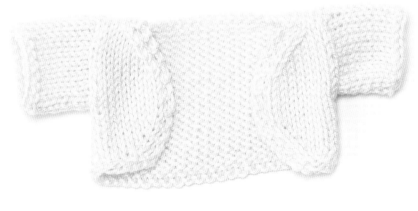

Making Up

Doll

See Making Up Your Doll in Techniques. Please follow the Bracelet instructions below before sewing up the left arm.

Bracelet

Stitch together (on ws), the first and last rows of Yarn E using an over stitch through the back loops **(A)**. Fasten off ends of Yarn E.

Pigtails

1. Sew together the small cast off edges using whip stitch (see Techniques).Thread the cast on tail through cast on stitches at bottom of pigtails and draw up. Sew side edges together, stuffing lightly as you go.

2. Sew pigtails on to each side of head and bury loose ends in head (see **B** for position of pigtails).

Hair scrunchie

Loop the i-cord over top of pigtail and secure ends with a couple of stitches **(B)**.

Clothing

Shrug

1. Block all the pieces of the shrug before making up.

2. Start by sewing up the shoulder seams, then sew the sleeves to the front and back pieces, lining up the centre of the sleeves to the shoulder seams.

3. Sew up the sleeve and body edge seams to finish.

Dress

1. Block all the pieces of the dress before making up.

2. Start by sewing the buttons into place on the back of the dress, matching them up with the button holes.

3. Sew up the shoulder seams, make sure you leave a big enough gap to fit around Grace's neck.

4. Matching up the stripes sew up the edge seams, leaving a 2½cm (1in) gap at the top for the armholes.

5. Picot hem: fold the hem back along the eyelet holes with wrong sides together, making sure stitches are in line. Working from the wrong side sew in place as follows: secure a length of Yarn C to back of work, insert needle through a back stitch loop **(C)**, then through its vertically matching cast on loop **(D)** and then down through the next cast on loop **(E)**. Pull yarn through and repeat until hem is complete.

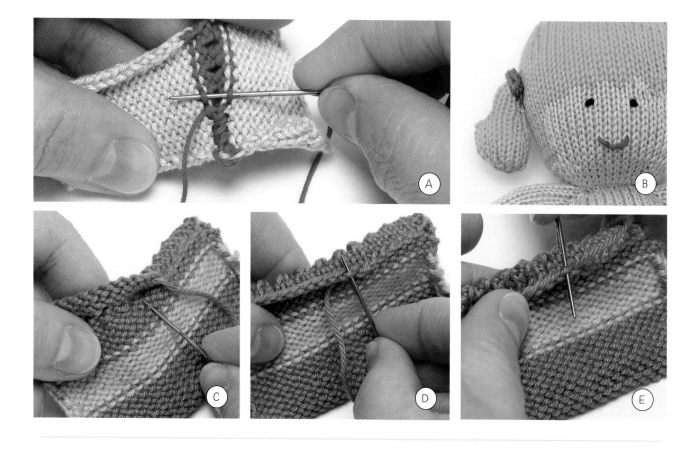

Ralph

A lot of little boys like trains but Ralph absolutely loves them. If he's not pushing wooden toy ones around a track, he's yearning to travel the rails on the real thing. A practical little chap, he wears dungarees with a handy pocket for tickets, timetables and the occasional sweetie. He likes to keep those smart little knee socks pulled up but no one can quite manage to tame that unruly tuft of hair.

You Will Need

Yarn

- **Yarn A** Beige
- **Yarn B** Brown
- **Yarn C** Petrol Blue
- **Yarn D** White
- **Yarn E** Pale Grey
- **Yarn F** Red
- **Yarn G** Camel
- Scraps of black and red for eyes and mouth

Finished Size

- 28cm (11in) tall

You will also need

- 3mm (US 2½) straight needles
- 2.5mm (US 1½) straight needles
- 2.5mm (US 1½) double-pointed needles
- Stitch holder
- Tapestry needle
- 3 x 15mm (½in) circles of white felt
- Toy stuffing
- 3 x 6mm (¼in) buttons

Pattern

Cast on using the Long-tail (double cast on) method (see Techniques) unless otherwise indicated. Where possible leave long tails when you cast on and cast off and use these for the sewing up.

Head

Using Yarn A and 2.5mm needles cast on 13 sts.

Starting at neck:

Row 1 (ws): Purl.

Row 2: [K1, M1] 12 times, K1. (25 sts)

Row 3: Purl.

Row 4: K3, [K1, M1] 7 times, K4, [K1, M1] 7 times, K4. (39 sts)

Rows 5–7: Stocking stitch 3 rows.

Row 8: K3, [K3, M1] 4 times, K6, [K3, M1] 4 times, K6. (47 sts)

Cut yarn.

Rows 9–31: Using Intarsia technique (see Techniques) and working in stocking stitch work Hair Chart. Start with a purl row (ws) at the bottom left hand corner of chart, read purl rows (ws) from left to right and knit rows (rs) from right to left.

For top of head continue in Yarn B.

Row 32: K8, K2tog, K4, SSK, K15, K2tog, K4, SSK, K8. (43 sts)

Row 33: Purl.

Row 34: K8, K2tog, K2, SSK, K15, K2tog, K2, SSK, K8. (39 sts)

Row 35: Purl.

Row 36: K8, K2tog, SSK, K15, K2tog, SSK, K8. (35 sts)

Cut yarn, transfer the stitches onto a stitch holder.

Hair tufts

(make 3)

Using 2.5mm double pointed needles and Yarn B cast on 3 sts and make an i-cord of 3 rows (see Techniques).

Body

T-SHIRT

Using Yarn D and 2.5mm needles cast on 9 sts.

Starting at neck:

Row 1 (ws): Purl.

Change to Yarn E.

Row 2: K1, [K1, M1] 6 times, K2. (15 sts)

Row 3: Purl.

Change to Yarn D.

Row 4: K2, [K1, M1] 3 times, K4, [K1, M1] 3 times, K3. (21 sts)

Row 5: Purl.

Continue working in stripe pattern of 2 rows Yarn E and 2 rows Yarn D for the next 22 rows.

Row 6: K3, [K1, M1] 4 times, K6, [K1, M1] 4 times, K4. (29 sts)

Rows 7–9: Stocking stitch 3 rows.

Row 10: K4, [K1, M1] 6 times, K8, [K1, M1] 6 times, K5. (41 sts)

Rows 11–15: Stocking stitch 5 rows.

Row 16: K3, [K3, M1] 4 times, K8, [K3, M1] 4 times, K6. (49 sts)

Rows 17–27: Stocking stitch 11 rows.

BOXER SHORTS

Continue working the 49 sts on needle.

Change to Yarn F.

Rows 28–30: Knit 3 rows.

Row 31: P22, K1, P2, K1, P23.

Row 32: Knit.

Rows 33–36: Rpt last 2 rows, 2 more times.

Row 37: P23, K3, P23.

Row 38: Knit.

Row 39: P25, K1, P23.

Row 40: Knit.

Rows 41–42: Rpt last 2 rows.

Row 43: P25, K1, P23.

Cast off.

Arms

(make 2)

Using Yarn A and 2.5mm needles cast on 12 sts.

Rows 1–3: Starting with a purl row (ws), stocking stitch 3 rows.

Row 4: Cast on 3 sts using Knit Cast-on method (see Techniques), knit to end. (15 sts)

Row 5: Cast on 3 sts using Purl Cast-on method (see Techniques), purl to end. (18 sts)

Rows 6–7: Stocking stitch 2 rows.

Row 8: SSK, K14, K2tog. (16 sts)

Row 9: Purl.

Row 10: SSK, K12, K2tog. (14 sts)

Row 11: Purl.

Row 12: SSK, K10, K2tog. (12 sts)

Row 13: Purl.

SLEEVES

Continue working the 12 sts on needle:

Change to Yarn F.

Rows 14–15: Knit 2 rows.

Change to Yarn D.

Rows 16–17: Stocking stitch 2 rows.

Change to Yarn E.

Rows 18–19: Stocking stitch 2 rows.

Continue in stripe pattern of 2 rows Yarn D and 2 rows Yarn E for remainder of arm.

Rows 20–47: Stocking stitch 28 rows.

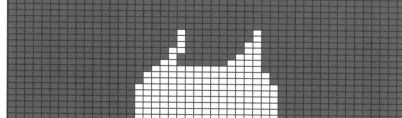

Hair Chart

☐ = Yarn A
■ = Yarn B

Row 48: SSK, K8, K2tog. (10 sts)

Row 49: Purl.

Row 50: SSK, K6, K2tog. (8 sts)

Row 51: Purl.

Row 52: SSK, K4, K2tog. (6 sts)

Row 53: Purl.

Row 54: SSK, K2, K2tog. (4 sts)

Row 55: Purl.

Cast off.

Legs and sneakers

(make 2)

Start at base of sneaker.

Using Yarn G and 2.5mm needles cast on 12 sts.

Row 1 (ws): Purl.

Row 2: K1, M1, K3, [K1, M1] 3 times, K4, M1, K1. (17 sts)

Row 3: Purl.

Row 4: [K1, M1] 2 times, K3, [K1, M1] 2 times, K2, [K1, M1] 2 times, K3, [K1, M1] 2 times, K1. (25 sts)

Row 5: Purl.

Row 6: [K2, M1] 2 times, K2, [K2, M1] 2 times, K3, [K2, M1] 2 times, K2, [K2, M1] 2 times, K2. (33 sts)

Row 7: Purl.

Change to Yarn D.

Row 8: [K3, M1] 2 times, K1, [K3, M1] 2 times, K4, [K3, M1] 2 times, K1, [K3, M1] 2 times, K3. (41 sts)

Row 9: Knit.

Row 10: Purl.

Use Intarsia technique (see Techniques) for changing yarn across the next 8 rows:

(D) = Use Yarn D.

(F) = Use Yarn F.

Row 11: (F) P14, (D) P13, (F) P14.

Row 12: (F) K14, (D) K13, (F) K14.

Row 13: (F) P14, (D) P13, (F) P14.

Row 14: (F) K14, (D) K1, SSK, K7, K2tog, K1, (F) K14. (39 sts)

Row 15: (F) P14, (D) P11, (F) P14.

Row 16: (F) K14, (D) K1, SSK, K5, K2tog, K1, (F) K14. (37 sts)

Row 17: (F) P14, (D) P9, (F) P14.

Row 18: (F) K7, (D) K8, SSK, K3, K2tog, K8, (F) K7. (35 sts)

Change to Yarn D.

Row 19: Purl.

Row 20: P8, [K7, SSK, K1, K2tog, K7] cast off these middle 17 sts as you work them, P to end. (16 sts)

Row 21: K7, P2tog, K7. (15 sts)

SOCKS

Continue working the 15 sts on needle.

Change to Yarn E.

Rows 22–33: Stocking stitch 12 rows.

Change to Yarn D.

Row 34: Knit.

Change to Yarn C.

Row 35: Purl.

Change to Yarn D.

Row 36: Knit.

Change to Yarn E.

Row 37: Purl.

Rows 38–41: Knit 4 rows.

TOP OF LEG

Continue working the 15 sts on needle.

Change to Yarn A.

Rows 42–71: Stocking stitch 30 rows.

BOXER SHORTS LEG

Continue working the 15 sts on needle.

Change to Yarn F.

Row 72: Knit.

Row 73: Knit.

Rows 74–77: Stocking stitch 4 rows.

Cast off.

Dungarees

Made in one piece and seamed at the inside leg and back of body.

Left leg of dungarees

Start at the bottom of left leg.

Using Yarn C and 3mm needles cast on 29 sts.

Rows 1–18: Starting with a purl row (ws), stocking stitch 18 rows.

Slip all stitches onto stitch holder.

Cut yarn.

Right leg of dungarees

Starting at the bottom of right leg.

Using Yarn C and 3mm needles cast on 29 sts.

Rows 1–18: Starting with a purl row (ws), stocking stitch 18 rows.

Row 19: Purl.

Leave these stitches on the right hand needle and do not cut the yarn.

JOIN LEGS OF DUNGAREES

Slip the stitches from the stitch holder back onto the LH knitting needle, purl to the end of the row. You should now have 58 sts on one needle.

Row 20: Knit.

Rows 21–34: Starting with a purl row (ws), stocking stitch 14 rows.

Row 35: P1, [K1, P2] 7 times, K2, P10, K2, [P2, K1] 7 times, P1. (58 sts)

Row 36: K1, [P1, K2] 7 times, K14, [K2, P1] 7 times, K1. (58 sts)

Rows 37–38: Rpt last 2 rows.

Row 39: P1, [K1, P2] 7 times, K2, P10, K2, [P2, K1] 7 times, P1. (58 sts)

Row 40: Cast off 22 sts in pattern, K14, Cast off 22 sts in pattern. (14 sts)

Cut yarn.

DUNGAREE BIB

Working on remaining 14 sts, rejoin yarn.

Row 41: K2, P10, K2.

Row 42: Knit.

Rows 43–52: Rpt last 2 rows, 5 more times.

Row 53: Knit.

Cast off knitwise.

Dungaree strap

(make 2)

Using Yarn C and 3mm needles cast on 28 sts.

Row 1 (ws): K25, P3.

Row 2: K3, turn.

Row 3: P3.

Cast off knitwise.

Pocket

Using Yarn C and 3mm needles cast on 8 sts.

Rows 1–5: Starting with a purl row (ws), stocking stitch 5 rows.

Row 6: Purl.

Cast off knitwise.

A

C

B

D

E

Making up

Doll

See Making Up Your Doll in Techniques. Please note:

1. Sew a small button on to the fly of the boxer shorts before sewing up the body (see **A** for position).

2. Using Duplicate stitch (see Techniques) embroider three white stripes onto each side of the sneakers before sewing up **(B)**.

Hair tufts

Sew the hair tufts on to the top corner of the completed head **(C)**.

Clothing

Dungarees

1. Before sewing together, block all the parts of the dungarees.

2. Sew the pocket onto the front of the bib, making sure it's central **(D)**.

3. Then sew up inside leg seams to crotch, followed by the back seam.

4. Sew the straps on to the back edge of the dungarees, around 2cm (¾in) either side of the back seam **(E)**. Sew the other end of the straps to the top corners of the bib and then sew on the buttons.

Penny

She's at her happiest in the park, whether it's swinging so high that her sun hat blows off or playing football with her friends, Penny would spend all day outdoors if she could. Her practical jeggings make climbing trees a breeze, and she can get to the highest branches, which is handy if you're trying to spot where on earth your hat landed.

You Will Need

Yarn

- **Yarn A** Mocha
- **Yarn B** Dark Brown
- **Yarn C** Cream
- **Yarn D** Pale Grey
- **Yarn E** White
- **Yarn F** Watermelon
- **Yarn G** Denim
- Scraps of black and red of eyes and mouth

Finished size

- 28cm (11in) tall

You will also need

- 3mm (US 2½) straight needles
- 2.5mm (US 1½) straight needles
- 2.5mm (US 1½) double-pointed needles
- Stitch holder
- Tapestry needle
- 3 x 15mm (½in) circles of white felt
- Toy stuffing
- 5 x 6mm (¼in) buttons
- Small piece of ribbon

Pattern

Cast on using the Long-tail (double cast on) method (see Techniques) unless otherwise indicated. Where possible leave long tails when you cast on and cast off and use these for the sewing up.

Head

Starting at neck:

Using Yarn A and 2.5mm needles cast on 13 sts.

Row 1 (ws): Purl.

Row 2: [K1, M1] 12 times, K1. (25 sts)

Row 3: Purl.

Row 4: K3, [K1, M1] 7 times, K4, [K1, M1] 7 times, K4. (39 sts)

Rows 5–7: Stocking stitch 3 rows.

Row 8: K3, [K3, M1] 4 times, K6, [K3, M1] 4 times, K6. (47 sts)

Cut yarn.

Rows 9–31: Using Intarsia technique (see Techniques) and working in stocking stitch work Hair Chart. Start with a purl row (ws) at the bottom left hand corner of chart, read purl rows (ws) from left to right and knit rows (rs) from right to left.

For top of head continue in Yarn B.

Row 32: K8, K2tog, K4, SSK, K15, K2tog, K4, SSK, K8. (43 sts)

Row 33: Purl.

Row 34: K8, K2tog, K2, SSK, K15, K2tog, K2, SSK, K8. (39 sts)

Row 35: Purl.

Row 36: K8, K2tog, SSK, K15, K2tog, SSK, K8. (35 sts)

Cut yarn, transfer the stitches onto a stitch holder.

Body

Using Yarn A and 2.5mm needles cast on 9 sts.

Starting at neck:

Row 1 (ws): Purl.

Row 2: K1, [K1, M1] 6 times, K2. (15 sts)

Row 3: Purl.

Row 4: K2, [K1, M1] 3 times, K4, [K1, M1] 3 times, K3. (21 sts)

Row 5: Purl.

Row 6: K3, [K1, M1] 4 times, K6, [K1, M1] 4 times, K4. (29 sts)

Rows 7–9: Stocking stitch 3 rows.

Row 10: K4, [K1, M1] 6 times, K8, [K1, M1] 6 times, K5. (41 sts)

Rows 11–15: Stocking stitch 5 rows.

Row 16: K3, [K3, M1] 4 times, K8, [K3, M1] 4 times, K6. (49 sts)

Rows 17–27: Stocking stitch 11 rows.

TOP OF JEGGINGS

Continue working the 49 sts on needle.

Change to Yarn G

Rows 28–29: Knit 2 rows.

Rows 30–43: Starting with a knit row, stocking stitch 14 rows.

Cast off.

Arms

(make 2)

Using Yarn A and 2.5mm needles cast on 12 sts.

Rows 1–3: Starting with a purl row (ws), stocking stitch 3 rows.

Row 4: Cast on 3 sts using Knit Cast-on method (see Techniques), knit to end. (15 sts)

Row 5: Cast on 3 sts using Purl Cast-on method (see Techniques), purl to end. (18 sts)

Rows 6–7: Stocking stitch 2 rows.

Row 8: SSK, K14, K2tog. (16 sts)

Row 9: Purl.

Row 10: SSK, K12, K2tog. (14 sts)

Row 11: Purl.

Row 12: SSK, K10, K2tog. (12 sts)

Rows 13–47: Stocking stitch 35 rows.

Row 48: SSK, K8, K2tog. (10 sts)

Row 49: Purl.

Row 50: SSK, K6, K2tog. (8 sts)

Row 51: Purl.

Row 52: SSK, K4, K2tog. (6 sts)

Row 53: Purl.

Row 54: SSK, K2, K2tog. (4 sts)

Row 55: Purl.

Cast off.

Legs and sneakers

(make 2)

Starting at base of sneaker:

Using Yarn D and 2.5mm needles cast on 12 sts.

Row 1 (ws): Purl.

Row 2: K1, M1, K3, (K1, M1) 3 times, K4, M1, K1. (17 sts)

Row 3: Purl.

Row 4: (K1, M1) 2 times, K3, (K1, M1) 2 times, K2, (K1, M1) 2 times, K3, (K1, M1) 2 times, K1. (25 sts)

Row 5: Purl.

Row 6: (K2, M1) 2 times, K2, (K2, M1) 2 times, K3, (K2, M1) 2 times, K2, (K2, M1) 2 times, K2. (33 sts)

Row 7: Purl.

Change to Yarn E.

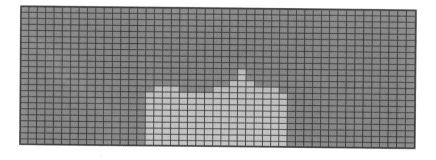

Hair Chart

□ = Yarn A   ■ = Yarn B

Row 8: (K3, M1) 2 times, K1, (K3, M1) 2 times, K4, (K3, M1) 2 times, K1, (K3, M1) 2 times, K3. (41 sts)

Row 9: Knit.

Row 10: Purl.

The next 8 rows use Intarsia technique (see Techniques) for changing yarns: (E) = Use Yarn E (F) = Use Yarn F

Row 11: (F) P14, (E) P13, (F) P14.

Row 12: (F) K14, (E) K13, (F) K14.

Row 13: (F) P14, (E) P13, (F) P14.

Row 14: (F) K14, (E) K1, SSK, K7, K2tog, K1, (F) K14. (39 sts)

Row 15: (F) P14, (E) P11, (F) P14.

Row 16: (F) K14, (E) K1, SSK, K5, K2tog, K1, (F) K14. (37 sts)

Row 17: (F) P14, (E) P9, (F) P14.

Row 18: (F) K7, (E) K8, SSK, K3, K2tog, K8, (F) K7. (35 sts)

Change to Yarn E.

Row 19: Purl.

Row 20: P8, [K7, SSK, K1, K2tog, K7] cast off these middle 17 sts as you work them, P to end. (16 sts)

Row 21: K7, P2tog, K7. (15 sts)

LEGS AND JEGGINGS

Continue working the 15 sts on needle: Change to Yarn A.

Row 22–27: Stocking stitch 6 rows.

Change to Yarn G.

Rows 28–29: Knit 2 rows.

Row 30–77: Starting with a knit row, stocking stitch 48 rows.

Cast off.

Dress

Front

Using Yarn E and 3mm needles cast on 55 sts.

Row 1 (ws): Purl.

Row 2: K1, [YO, SSK, K1, K2tog, YO, K1] to end.

Row 3: Purl.

Row 4: K2, [YO, Sl1, K2tog, PSSO, YO, K3] to last 5 sts, YO, Sl1, K2tog, PSSO, YO, K2.

Rows 5–7: Stocking stitch 3 rows.

Row 8: [K1, K2tog] to last st, K1. (37 sts)

Change to Yarn C.

Rows 9–10: Purl 2 rows.

Starting with Yarn D, the dress is now worked in a stripe pattern of 2 rows Yarn D and 4 rows Yarn C, throughout.

Rows 11–39: Starting with a purl row, stocking stitch 29 rows.

Row 40: [K1, K2tog] to last st, K1. (25 sts)

Row 41: Purl.

Row 42: K1, SSK, K19, K2tog, K1. (23 sts)

Row 43: Purl.

Row 44: K1, SSK, K17, K2tog, K1. (21 sts)

Row 45: Purl.

Row 46: K1, SSK, K15, K2tog, K1. (19 sts)

Rows 47–57: Stocking stitch 11 rows.

Cast off.

Back

Using Yarn E and 3mm needles cast on 55 sts.

Row 1 (ws): Purl.

Row 2: K1, [YO, SSK, K1, K2tog, YO, K1] to end.

Row 3: Purl.

Row 4: K2, [YO, Sl1, K2tog, PSSO, YO, K3] to last 5 sts, YO, Sl1, K2tog, PSSO, YO, K2.

Rows 5–7: Stocking stitch 3 rows.

Row 8: [K1, K2tog] to last st, K1. (37 sts)

Change to Yarn C

Rows 9–10: Purl 2 rows.

Rows 11–43 are worked in a stripe pattern of 2 rows Yarn D and 4 rows Yarn C, starting with Yarn D.

Rows 11–39: Stocking stitch 29 rows.

Row 40: [K1, K2tog] to last st, K1. (25 sts)

Row 41: Purl.

Row 42: K1, SSK, K19, K2tog, K1. (23 sts)

Row 43: Purl.

RIGHT BUTTON PLACKET

Continue in Yarn C.

Row 44: K1, SSK, K10, turn. (12 sts)

Row 45: K3, P9.

Row 46: K1, SSK, K9, turn. (11 sts)

Row 47: K3, P8.

Row 48: K9, YO, K2tog, turn.

Row 49: K1, Ktbl, K1, P8.

Row 50: K11, turn.

Row 51: K3, P8.

Rows 52–55: Rpt last 2 rows, 2 more times.

Row 56: K9, YO, K2tog, turn.

Row 57: K1, Ktbl, K1, P8.

Cast off 11 sts, cut yarn.

LEFT BUTTON PLACKET

Row 1: Returning to stitches still on needle, rejoin Yarn C and pick up and knit 3 sts from BEHIND the first row of Right Button Placket (see Techniques, Picking Up Stitches), knit across stitches on left hand needle to last 3 sts, K2tog, K1. (12 sts)

Row 2: P9, K3.

Row 3: K9, K2tog, K1. (11 sts)

Row 4: P8, K3.

Row 5: Knit.

Rows 6–13: Rpt last 2 rows, 4 more times.

Row 14: P8, K3.

Cast off.

Sleeves

(make 2)

Using Yarn F and 3mm needles cast on 20 sts.

Row 1 (ws): Knit.

Starting with Yarn C, the sleeves are now worked in a stripe pattern of 4 rows Yarn C and 2 rows Yarn D, throughout.

Rows 2–15: Starting with a knit row, stocking stitch 14 rows.

Cast off.

Pocket

Using Yarn F and 3mm needles cast on 7 sts.

Row 1 (ws): Purl.

Rows 2–6: Stocking stitch 5 rows.

Row 7: Knit.

Cast off.

Hat

Using Yarn D and 3mm needles cast on 75 sts.

Row 1 (ws): Knit.

Rows 2–7: Starting with a knit row, stocking stitch 6 rows.

Row 8: [K1, K2tog] to end. (50 sts)

Row 9: Knit.

Rows 10–21: Stocking stitch 12 rows.

Row 22: [K3, K2tog] to end. (40 sts)

Row 23: Purl.

Row 24: [K2, K2tog] to end. (30 sts)

Row 25: Purl.

Row 26: [K1, K2tog] to end. (20 sts)

Row 27: Purl.

Row 28: [K2tog] to end. (10 sts)

Cut yarn leaving a long tail, using a tapestry needle thread tail through the stitches left on needle and draw up.

Making Up

Doll

See Making Up Your Doll in Techniques.

Plaits

(make 2)

1. See Making Plaits in Techniques.
2. Sew plaits to each side of the head and finish of with a small piece of ribbon **(A)**.

Clothing & Accessories

Dress

1. Block all the pieces of the dress before making up.

2. Start by sewing the buttons into place on the back of the dress, matching them up with the button holes **(B)**
3. Sew the pocket onto the front of dress **(C)**.
4. Sew up the shoulder seams, making sure you leave a big enough gap to fit around Penny's neck.
5. Sew sleeves to front and back pieces lining up centre of sleeves to shoulder seams. Matching up the stripes sew up the sleeve and dress edge seams.

Hat

Sew the edges of the hat together then sew three tiny buttons to the front to finish **(D)**.

A

B

C

D

Faye

Faye's whole world revolves around bunnies, and she dreams of the day when she might be allowed to have a furry long-eared friend of her own. It's no surprise then that when choosing an outfit for a party she insisted on *that* hat and *that* pink dress. When the cake arrives she'll giggle her way through 'hoppy birthday to you'!

You Will Need

Yarn

Yarn A Beige

Yarn B Cream

Yarn C Charcoal

Yarn D White

Yarn E Pink

Yarn F Black

Yarn G Pale Pink

Scraps of black and red for eyes and mouth

Finished size

28cm (11in) tall

You will also need

3mm (US 2½) straight needles

2.5mm (US 1½) straight needle

2.5mm (US 1½) double-pointed needles

Stitch holder

Tapestry needle

3 x 15mm (½in) circles of white felt

Toy stuffing

2 x 6mm (¼in) buttons

Pattern

Cast on using the Long-tail (double cast on) method (see Techniques) unless otherwise indicated. Where possible leave long tails when you cast on and cast off and use these for the sewing up.

Head

Using Yarn A and 2.5mm needles cast on 13 sts.

Starting at neck:

Row 1 (ws): Purl.

Row 2: [K1, M1] 12 times, K1. (25 sts)

Row 3: Purl.

Row 4: K3, [K1, M1] 7 times, K4, [K1, M1] 7 times, K4. (39 sts)

Rows 5–7: Stocking stitch 3 rows.

Row 8: K3, [K3, M1] 4 times, K6, [K3, M1] 4 times, K6. (47 sts)

Cut yarn.

Rows 9–31: Using Intarsia technique (see Techniques) and working in stocking stitch work Hair Chart. Start with a purl row (ws) at the bottom left hand corner of chart, read purl rows (ws) from left to right and knit rows (rs) from right to left.

For top of head continue in Yarn B.

Row 32: K8, K2tog, K4, SSK, K15, K2tog, K4, SSK, K8. (43 sts)

Row 33: Purl.

Row 34: K8, K2tog, K2, SSK, K15, K2tog, K2, SSK, K8. (39 sts)

Row 35: Purl.

Row 36: K8, K2tog, SSK, K15, K2tog, SSK, K8. (35 sts)

Cut yarn, transfer the stitches onto a stitch holder.

Pigtails

(make 2)

Using Yarn B and 3mm needles cast on 64 sts.

Row 1: [K1, cast off next 20 sts] rpt to last st, K1. (4 sts)

Cut the yarn leaving a long tail, using a tapestry needle thread the tail through the 4 stitches left on the needle and draw up **(A and B)**.

Body

T-SHIRT

Using Yarn D and 2.5mm needles cast on 9 sts.

Starting at neck:

Row 1 (ws): Purl.

Row 2: K1, [K1, M1] 6 times, K2. (15 sts)

Row 3: Purl.

Row 4: K2, [K1, M1] 3 times, K4, [K1, M1] 3 times, K3. (21 sts)

Row 5: Purl.

Row 6: K3, [K1, M1] 4 times, K6, [K1, M1] 4 times, K4. (29 sts)

Rows 7–9: Stocking stitch 3 rows.

Row 10: K4, [K1, M1] 6 times, K8, [K1, M1] 6 times, K5. (41 sts)

Rows 11–15: Stocking stitch 5 rows.

Row 16: K3, [K3, M1] 4 times, K8, [K3, M1] 4 times, K6. (49 sts)

Rows 17–27: Stocking stitch 11 rows.

TOP OF TIGHTS

Continue working the 49 sts on needle.

Starting with Yarn C, the tights are worked in a stripe pattern of 2 rows each of Yarn C and Yarn D throughout.

Rows 28–29: Knit 2 rows.

Rows 30–43: Starting with a knit row stocking stitch 14 rows.

Cast off.

Arms

(make 2)

Using Yarn A and 2.5mm needles cast on 12 sts.

Rows 1–3: Starting with a purl row (ws), stocking stitch 3 rows.

Row 4: Cast on 3 sts using Knit Cast-on method (see Techniques), knit to end. (15 sts)

Row 5: Cast on 3 sts using Purl Cast-on method (see Techniques), purl to end. (18 sts)

Rows 6–7: Stocking stitch 2 rows.

Row 8: SSK, K14, K2tog. (16 sts)

Row 9: Purl.

Row 10: SSK, K12, K2tog. (14 sts)

Row 11: Purl.

Row 12: SSK, K10, K2tog. (12 sts)

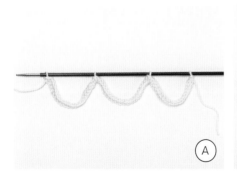

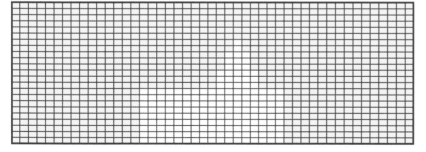

Hair Chart

□ = Yarn A
□ = Yarn B

SLEEVES

Continue working the 12 sts on needle:

Change to Yarn D.

Rows 13–14: Purl 2 rows.

Rows 15–47: Starting with a purl row, stocking stitch 33 rows.

Row 48: SSK, K8, K2tog. (10 sts)

Row 49: Purl.

Row 50: SSK, K6, K2tog. (8 sts)

Row 51: Purl.

Row 52: SSK, K4, K2tog. (6 sts)

Row 53: Purl.

Row 54: SSK, K2, K2tog. (4 sts)

Row 55: Purl.

Cast off.

Legs and boots

(make 2)

Starting at sole of boot:

Using Yarn F and 2.5mm needles cast on 12 sts.

Row 1 (ws): Purl.

Row 2: K1, M1, K3, (K1, M1) 3 times, K4, M1, K1. (17 sts)

Row 3: Purl.

Row 4: (K1, M1) 2 times, K3, (K1, M1) 2 times, K2, (K1, M1) 2 times, K3, (K1, M1) 2 times, K1. (25 sts)

Row 5: Purl.

Row 6: (K2, M1) 2 times, K2, (K2, M1) 2 times, K3, (K2, M1) 2 times, K2, (K2, M1) 2 times, K2. (33 sts)

Row 7: Purl.

Row 8: (K3, M1) 2 times, K1, (K3, M1) 2 times, K4, (K3, M1) 2 times, K1, (K3, M1) 2 times, K3. (41 sts)

Row 9: Knit.

Row 10: Purl.

Change to Yarn C.

Rows 11–13: Starting with a purl row, stocking stitch 3 rows.

Row 14: K15, SSK, K7, K2tog, K15. (39 sts)

Row 15: Purl.

Row 16: K15, SSK, K5, K2tog, K15. (37 sts)

Row 17: Purl.

Row 18: K15, SSK, K3, K2tog, K15. (35 sts)

Row 19: Purl.

Row 20: K8, [K7, SSK, K1, K2tog, K7] cast off these middle 17 sts as you work them, K to end. (16 sts)

Row 21: P7, P2tog, P7. (15 sts)

BOTTOM OF TIGHTS

Continue working the 15 sts on needle.

Starting with Yarn D, the tights are worked in a stripe pattern of 2 rows each of Yarn D and Yarn C throughout.

Rows 22–77: Stocking stitch 56 rows.

Cast off using Yarn D.

Boot cuff

(make 2)

Using Yarn C and 3mm needles cast on 31 sts.

Starting at the top of the cuff.

Row 1 (ws): [P1, K2] to last st, P1.

Row 2: [K1, P2] to last st, K1.

Row 3–18: Rpt last 2 rows, 8 more times.

Row 19: [P1, K2tog] to last st, P1. (21 sts)

Row 20: [K1, P1] to last st, K1.

Row 21: [P1, K1] to last st, P1.

Row 22–27: Rpt last 2 rows, 3 more times.

Row 28: [K1, P1] to last st, K1.

Cast off.

Dress
Front of dress

Using Yarn E and 3mm needles cast on 49 sts.

Row 1–7: Starting with a purl row (ws), stocking stitch 7 rows.

Row 8: K2, [K2tog, K4] 7 times, K2tog, K3. (41 sts)

Row 9: Purl.

Row 10: K1, [K3, K2tog] to end. (33 sts)

Rows 11–12: Purl 2 rows.

Dress chart A is placed in the following rows using Intarsia technique (see Techniques) and worked in stocking stitch. Starting at the bottom left-hand corner of chart, read purl rows (ws) from left to right and knit rows (rs) from right to left.

Row 13: P9, work Dress Chart A, P5.

Row 14: K5, work Dress Chart A, K9.

Rows 15–18: Repeat last 2 rows, 2 more times.

Row 19: P9, work Dress Chart A, P5.

Row 20: K2tog, K3, work Dress Chart A, K7, K2tog. (31 sts)

Row 21: P8, work Dress Chart A, P4.

Row 22: K4, work Dress Chart A, K8.

Rows 23–24: Repeat last 2 rows.

Row 25: P8, work Dress Chart A, P4.

Row 26: K2tog, K2, work Dress Chart A, K6, K2tog. (29 sts)

Row 27: P7, work Dress Chart A, P3.

Row 28: K3, work Dress Chart A, K7.

Rows 29–30: Repeat last 2 rows.

Row 31: P7, work Dress Chart A, P3.

Row 32: K2tog, K1, work Dress Chart A, K5, K2tog. (27 sts)

Row 33: P6, work Dress Chart A, P2.

Row 34: K2, work Dress Chart A, K6.

Rows 35–36: Repeat last 2 rows.

Row 37: P6, work Dress Chart A, P2.

Row 38: K2tog, work Dress Chart A, K4, K2tog. (25 sts)

Row 39: P5, work Dress Chart A, P1.

Row 40: K1, work Dress Chart A, K5.

Rows 41–42: Repeat last 2 rows.

Row 43: P5, work Dress Chart A, P1

Row 44: K2tog, Knit to last 2 sts, K2tog. (23 sts)

Row 45: Purl.

Row 46: K2tog, Knit to last 2 sts, K2tog. (21 sts)

Rows 47–57: Stocking stitch 11 rows. Cast off.

Back of dress

Using Yarn E and 3mm needles cast on 49 sts.

Row 1–7: Starting with a purl row (ws), stocking stitch 7 rows.

Row 8: K2, [K2tog, K4] 7 times, K2tog, K3. (41 sts)

Row 9: Purl.

Row 10: K1, [K3, K2tog] to end. (33 sts)

Rows 11–12: Purl 2 rows.

Rows 13–19: Starting with a purl row, stocking stitch 7 rows.

Row 20: K2tog, knit to last 2 sts, K2tog. (31 sts)

Rows 21–25: Stocking stitch 5 rows.

Row 26: K2tog, knit to last 2 sts, K2tog. (29 sts)

Rows 27–31: Stocking stitch 5 rows.

Row 32: K2tog, knit to last 2 sts, K2tog. (27 sts)

Rows 33–37: Stocking stitch 5 rows.

Row 38: K2tog, knit to last 2 sts, K2tog. (25 sts)

Rows 39–43: Stocking stitch 5 rows.

RIGHT BUTTON PLACKET

Row 44: K2tog, K12, turn. (13 sts)

Row 45: K3, P10.

Row 46: K2tog, K11, turn. (12 sts)

Row 47: K3, P9.

Row 48: K10, YO, K2tog, turn.

Row 49: K1, Ktbl, K1, P9.

Row 50: K12, turn.

Row 51: K3, P9.

Rows 52–55: Rpt last 2 rows, 2 more times.

Row 56: K10, YO, K2tog, turn.

Row 57: K1, Ktbl, K1, P9.

Cast off 12 sts, cut yarn.

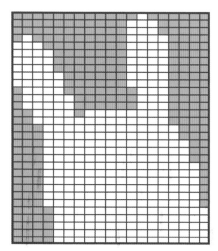

Dress Chart A

◨ = Yarn E ☐ = Yarn D

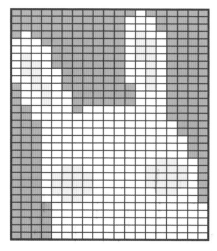

Dress Chart B

◨ = Yarn E ☐ = Yarn D ☐ = Yarn G

LEFT BUTTON PLACKET

Row 1: Returning to stitches still on needle, rejoin Yarn E and pick up and knit 3 sts from behind the first row of right button placket (see Techniques, Picking Up Stitches), knit across stitches on left-hand needle to last 2 sts, K2tog. (13 sts)

Row 2: P10, K3.

Row 3: Knit to last 2 sts, K2tog. (12 sts)

Row 4: P9, K3.

Row 5: Knit.

Rows 6–13: Rpt last 2 rows, 4 more times.

Row 14: P9, K3.

Cast off.

Sleeves

(make 2)

Using Yarn E and 2.5mm needles cast on 20 sts.

Row 1 (ws): [P2, K1] to last 2 sts, P2.

Row 2: [K2, P1] to last 2 sts, K2.

Rows 3–6: Rpt last 2 rows, 2 more times.

Change to 3mm needles.

Rows 7–11: Starting with a purl row, stocking stitch 5 rows.

Cast off.

Bunny hat

Hat

Using Yarn C and 3mm needles cast on 50 sts.

Rows 1 (ws): Knit.

Rows 2–4: Knit 3 rows.

Rows 5–15: Starting with a purl row, stocking stitch 11 rows.

Row 16: K4, [K2tog, K8] to last 4 sts, K4. (45 sts)

Row 17: Purl.

Row 18: K3, [K2tog, K7] to last 4 sts, K4. (40 sts)

Row 19: Purl.

Row 20: K2, [K2tog, K6] to last 4 sts, K4. (35 sts)

Row 21: Purl.

Row 22: K1, [K2tog, K5] to last 4 sts, K4. (30 sts)

Row 23: Purl.

Row 24: [K2tog, K4] to end. (25 sts)

Row 25: Purl.

Row 26: K2tog, to last st, K1. (13 sts)

Cut yarn leaving a long tail, using a tapestry needle thread tail through the stitches left on needle and draw up.

Hat ears

(make 2)

Using Yarn C and 3mm needles cast on 12 sts.

Row 1 (ws): [K1, P1] to end.

Row 2: [P1, K1] to end.

Rows 3–10: Rpt last 2 rows, 4 more times.

Row 11: [K1, P1] to end.

Row 12: [P1, K1] 2 times, P2tog, K2tog, [P1, K1] 2 times. (10sts)

Row 13: [K1, P1] to end.

Row 14: [P1, K1] to end.

Rows 15–16: Rpt last 2 rows.

Row 17: K1, P1, K1, P2tog, K2tog, P1, K1, P1. (8 sts)

Row 18: [P1, K1] to end.

Row 19: [K1, P1] to end.

Row 20: P1, K1, P2tog, K2tog, P1, K1. (6 sts)

Row 21: K1, P2tog, K2tog, P1. (4 sts)

Row 22: P2tog, K2tog. (2 sts)

Row 23: P2tog. (1 st)

Making Up

Doll

See Making Up Your Doll in Techniques.

Pigtails

Twist the three loops together so they lie on top of each other, and sew in place on either side of the head (C).

Clothing & Accessories

Dress

1. Using Dress Chart B, work the bunny's ears and cheeks in duplicate stitch (Swiss darning) with Yarn G (see Techniques).

2. Using a length of Yarn C, embroider the bunny's eyes, nose and mouth, using figure D as a guide.

3. Block all the pieces of the dress before continuing to make it up.

4. Sew buttons in place, on the left button placket (E).

5. Sew up the shoulder seams leaving a big enough gap to fit around neck. Sew the sleeves to the front and back pieces, lining up the centre of sleeves to shoulder seams.

6. Sew up the sleeve and dress edge seams.

Bunny hat

1. Sew the side edges of the hat together.

2. Weave in the ear cast-off tail down the edge of the ears, on the wrong side of the work (F).

3. With wrong sides facing, fold the ears in half. Thread the cast-on tail through the cast-on stitches and gather up (G and H).

4. Sew the ears to the top of the hat, making sure the seam of the hat is central at the back.

5. Thread any loose ends through to the wrong side of the hat and weave in.

Polly

Polly has three older brothers so she's learned to stand up for herself. Luckily she's never been very princess-y and would rather sling a few toy cars in her bag and head out for an adventure. If you don't want your pigtails pulled you have to adapt, and Polly's practical shorts, tights and ankle boots mean she can run like the wind.

You Will Need

Yarn

- **Yarn A** Beige
- **Yarn B** Camel
- **Yarn C** Cream
- **Yarn D** Orange
- **Yarn E** Sky Blue
- **Yarn F** Petrol Blue
- Scraps of black and red for eyes and mouth

Finished size

- 28cm (11in) tall

You will also need

- 3mm (US 2½) straight needles
- 2.5mm (US 1½) straight needles
- 2.5mm (US 1½) double-pointed needles
- Stitch holder
- Stitch markers
- Tapestry needle
- 3 x 15mm (½in) circles of white felt
- Toy stuffing
- 5 x 6mm (¼in) buttons

Pattern

Cast on using the Long-tail (double cast on) method (see Techniques) unless otherwise indicated. Where possible leave long tails when you cast on and cast off and use these for the sewing up.

Head

Starting at neck:

Using Yarn A and 2.5mm needles cast on 13 sts.

Row 1 (ws): Purl.

Row 2: [K1, M1] 12 times, K1. (25 sts)

Row 3: Purl.

Row 4: K3, [K1, M1] 7 times, K4, [K1, M1] 7 times, K4. (39 sts)

Rows 5–7: Stocking stitch 3 rows.

Row 8: K3, [K3, M1] 4 times, K6, [K3, M1] 4 times, K6. (47 sts)

Cut yarn.

Rows 9–31: Using Intarsia technique (see Techniques) and working in stocking stitch work Hair Chart. Start with a purl row (ws) at the bottom left hand corner of chart, read purl rows (ws) from left to right and knit rows (rs) from right to left.

For top of head continue in Yarn B.

Row 32: K8, K2tog, K4, SSK, K15, K2tog, K4, SSK, K8. (43 sts)

Row 33: Purl.

Row 34: K8, K2tog, K2, SSK, K15, K2tog, K2, SSK, K8. (39 sts)

Row 35: Purl.

Row 36: K8, K2tog, SSK, K15, K2tog, SSK, K8. (35 sts)

Cut yarn, transfer the stitches onto a stitch holder.

Body

T-SHIRT

Using Yarn E and 2.5mm needles cast on 9 sts.

Starting at neck:

Row 1 (ws): Purl.

Row 2: K1, [K1, M1] 6 times, K2. (15 sts)

Row 3: Purl.

Row 4: K2, [K1, M1] 3 times, K4, [K1, M1] 3 times, K3. (21 sts)

Row 5: Purl.

Row 6: K3, [K1, M1] 4 times, K6, [K1, M1] 4 times, K4. (29 sts)

Rows 7–9: Stocking stitch 3 rows.

Row 10: K4, [K1, M1] 6 times, K8, [K1, M1] 6 times, K5. (41 sts)

Rows 11–15: Stocking stitch 5 rows.

Row 16: K3, [K3, M1] 4 times, K8, [K3, M1] 4 times, K6. (49 sts)

Rows 17–27: Stocking stitch 11 rows.

TOP OF TIGHTS

Continue working the 49 sts on needle.

Starting with Yarn C, the tights are worked in a stripe pattern of 2 rows Yarn C and 2 rows Yarn E throughout.

Rows 28–29: Knit 2 rows.

Rows 30–43: Starting with a knit row, stocking stitch 14 rows.

Cast off.

Arms

(make 2)

Using Yarn A and 2.5mm needles cast on 12 sts.

Rows 1–3: Starting with a purl row (ws), stocking stitch 3 rows.

Row 4: Cast on 3 sts using knit cast-on method (see Techniques section), knit to end. (15 sts)

Row 5: Cast on 3 sts using purl cast-on method (see Techniques section), purl to end. (18 sts)

Rows 6–7: Stocking stitch 2 rows.

Row 8: SSK, K14, K2tog. (16 sts)

Row 9: Purl.

Row 10: SSK, K12, K2tog. (14 sts)

Row 11: Purl.

Row 12: SSK, K10, K2tog. (12 sts)

Rows 13–18: Stocking stitch 6 rows.

SLEEVES

Continue working the 12 sts on needle.

Change to Yarn E.

Rows 19–20: Purl 2 rows.

Rows 21–47: Starting with a purl row, stocking stitch 27 rows.

Row 48: SSK, K8, K2tog. (10 sts)

Row 49: Purl.

Row 50: SSK, K6, K2tog. (8 sts)

Row 51: Purl.

Row 52: SSK, K4, K2tog. (6 sts)

Row 53: Purl.

Row 54: SSK, K2, K2tog. (4 sts)

Row 55: Purl.

Cast off.

Legs and boots

(make 2)

Starting at sole of boot:

Using Yarn B and 2.5mm needles cast on 12 sts.

Row 1 (ws): Purl.

Row 2: K1, M1, K3, (K1, M1) 3 times, K4, M1, K1. (17 sts)

Row 3: Purl.

Row 4: (K1, M1) 2 times, K3, (K1, M1) 2 times, K2, (K1, M1) 2 times, K3, (K1, M1) 2 times, K1. (25 sts)

Row 5: Purl.

Row 6: (K2, M1) 2 times, K2, (K2, M1) 2 times, K3, (K2, M1) 2 times, K2, (K2, M1) 2 times, K2. (33 sts)

Row 7: Purl.

Hair Chart

□ = Yarn A
▨ = Yarn B

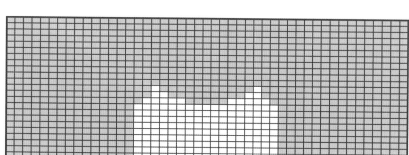

Row 8: (K3, M1) 2 times, K1, (K3, M1) 2 times, K4, (K3, M1) 2 times, K1, (K3, M1) 2 times, K3. (41 sts)

Row 9: Knit.

Row 10: Purl.

Rows 11–13: Starting with a purl row, stocking stitch 3 rows.

Row 14: K15, SSK, K7, K2tog, K15. (39 sts)

Row 15: Purl.

Row 16: K15, SSK, K5, K2tog, K15. (37 sts)

Row 17: Purl.

Row 18: K15, SSK, K3, K2tog, K15. (35 sts)

Row 19: Purl.

Row 20: K8, [K7, SSK, K1, K2tog, K7] cast off these middle 17 sts as you work them, K to end. (16 sts)

Row 21: P7, P2tog, P7. (15 sts)

BOTTOM OF TIGHTS

Continue working the 15 sts on needle.

Starting with Yarn E, the tights are worked in a stripe pattern of 2 rows each of Yarn E and Yarn C throughout.

Rows 22–77: Stocking stitch 56 rows.

Cast off using Yarn E.

Boot cuffs

(make 2)

Start at the top of the cuff.

Using Yarn C and 3mm needles cast on 31 sts.

Row 1 (ws): (P1, K2) to last st, P1.

Row 2: (K1, P2) to last st, K1.

Rows 3–12: Rpt last 2 rows, 5 more times.

Row 13: (P1, K2tog) to last st, P1. (21 sts)

Row 14: (K1, P1) to last st, K1.

Row 15: (P1, K1) to last st, P1.

Rows 16–20: Rpt last 2 rows, 2 more times, then rpt row 14 once more.

Cast off in pattern.

Tunic

The tunic is worked from the top down in one piece and fastened down the back. The button bands (first and last 3 sts on each row) are worked in Yarn C throughout, using Intarsia method (see Techniques). Colour changes along rows are indicated in ( ).

(C) = Use Yarn C   (D) = Use Yarn D
(E) = Use Yarn E

Using Yarn C and 3mm needles cast on 31 sts.

Row 1 (ws): K7, pm, K4, pm, K10, pm, K4, pm, K6.

Row 2: K1, YO, K2tog, [K to marker, m1r, sm, K1, m1l] 4 times, K to end. (39 sts)

Row 3: K3, purl to last 3 sts, K1, Ktbl, K1.

Row 4: [K to marker, m1r, sm, K1, m1l] 4 times, K to end. (47 sts)

Row 5: Rpt row 3.

Row 6: Rpt row 4. (55 sts)

Row 7: Rpt row 3.

Row 8: Rpt row 4. (63 sts)

Row 9: Rpt row 3.

Row 10: Rpt row 2. (71 sts)

Row 11: Rpt row 3.

Row 12: Rpt row 4. (79 sts)

Row 13: Rpt row 3.

Row 14: Rpt row 4. (87 sts)

The stitch markers are no longer needed.

Row 15: K3, P11, K17, P25, K17, P11, K3.

Row 16: K14, cast off 17 sts, K25, cast off 17 sts, K to end. (53 sts)

Row 17: K3, Pfb, [P2, Pfb] 3 times, [Pfb] 2 times, [P2, Pfb] 8 times, [Pfb] 2 times, [P2, Pfb] 3 times, K3. (72 sts)

Row 18: K1, YO, K2tog, knit to end.

Row 19: (C) K3, (D) purl to last 3 sts, (C) K1, Ktbl, K1.

Row 20: (C) K3, (D) K2, *YO, K3, pass first of the 3 knit sts over the 2nd and

3rd sts; rpt from * to last 4 sts, K1, (C) K3.

Rows 21: K3, purl to last 3 sts, K3.

Row 22: K4, *K3, pass first of the 3 knit sts over the 2nd and 3rd sts, YO; rpt from * to last 5 sts, K5.

Row 23: (C) K3, (E) purl to last 3 sts, (C) K3.

Row 24: (C) K3, (E) K2, *YO, K3, pass first of the 3 knit sts over the 2nd and 3rd sts; rpt from * to last 4 sts, K1, (C) K3.

Row 25: (C) K3, (D) purl to last 3 sts, (C) K3.

Row 26: (C) K1, YO, K2tog, (D) K1, *K3, pass first of the 3 knit sts over the 2nd and 3rd sts, YO; rpt from * to last 5 sts, K2, (C) K3.

Row 27: K3, purl to last 3 sts, K1, Ktbl, K1.

Row 28: K5, *YO, K3, pass first of the 3 knit sts over the 2nd and 3rd sts; rpt from * to last 4 sts, K4.

Row 29: (C) K3, (E) purl to last 3 sts, (C) K3.

Row 30: (C) K3, (E) K1, *K3, pass first of the 3 knit sts over the 2nd and 3rd sts, YO; rpt from * to last 5 sts, K2, (C) K3.

Row 31: (C) K3, (D) purl to last 3 sts, (C) K3.

Row 32: (C) K3, (D) K2, *YO, K3, pass first of the 3 knit sts over the 2nd and 3rd sts; rpt from * to last 4 sts, K1, (C) K3.

Row 33: K3, purl to last 3 sts, K3.

Row 34: K1, YO, K2tog, K1, *K3, pass first of the 3 knit sts over the 2nd and 3rd sts, YO; rpt from * to last 5 sts, K5.

Row 35: (C) K3, (E) purl to last 3 sts, (C) K1, Ktbl, K1.

Row 36: (C) K3, (E) K2, *YO, K3, pass first of the 3 knit sts over the 2nd and 3rd sts; rpt from * to last 4 sts, K1, (C) K3.

Row 37: (C) K3, (D) purl to last 3 sts, (C) K3.

Row 38: (C) K3, (D) K1, *K3, pass first of the 3 knit sts over the 2nd and 3rd sts, YO; rpt from * to last 5 sts, K2, (C) K3.

Row 39: K3, purl to last 3 sts, K3.

Rows 40–43: Knit 4 rows.

Cast off.

Shorts

Made in one piece and seamed at the inside leg and back of body.

Left leg

Starting at the bottom of left leg:

Using Yarn F and 3mm needles cast on 23 sts.

Row 1 (ws): Knit.

Rows 2–3: Knit 2 rows.

Rows 4–17: Starting with a knit row, stocking stitch 14 rows.

Row 18: Kfb, K to last st, Kfb. (25 sts)

Slip all stitches onto a stitch holder.

Cut yarn leaving a small tail to weave in later.

Right leg

Work rows 1–18 as left leg.

Row 19: Purl.

Leave these stitches on the right hand needle and do not cut the yarn.

JOIN LEGS

Slip the stitches from the stitch holder back onto the left hand knitting needle, purl to the end of the row. You should now have 50 sts on the needle.

Rows 20–34: Stocking stitch 15 rows.

Rows 35–37: Knit 3 rows.

Cast off.

Shopper bag

Bag

Using Yarn D and 3mm needles cast on 22 sts.

Row 1 (ws): *[Pfb] twice, P7, [Pfb] twice; rpt from * to end. (30 sts)

Row 2: K2, *YO, K3, pass first of the 3 knit sts over the 2nd and 3rd sts; rpt from * to last st, K1.

Row 3: Purl.

Row 4: K1, *K3, pass first of the 3 knit sts over the 2nd and 3rd sts, YO; rpt from * to last 2 sts, K2.

Row 5: Purl.

Rows 6–14: Rpt the last 4 rows, 2 more times, then rpt row 2 once more.

Row 15: Purl.

Row 16: K2, [K2tog, K2] to end. (23 sts)

Rows 17–19: Stocking stitch 3 rows.

Cast off.

Handle

Using Yarn D and 3mm needles cast on 70 sts.

Row 1 (ws): Knit and cast off all stitches.

Making Up

Doll

See Making Up Your Doll in Techniques.

Plaits

(make 2)

1. See Making Up Plaits in Techniques.

2. Sew plaits to top of head (see **A** for placement).

Clothing & Accessories

Tunic

1. Block the tunic before making up.

2. Sew the buttons into place on the back of the tunic, matching them up with the button holes **(B)**

Shorts

1. Block the shorts before making up.

2. Sew up the inside leg seams to crotch, followed by the back seam.

Shopper bag

1. Block the bag pieces before you make up.

2. Start by sewing the side and bottom edges of bag together.

3. Then attach each end of the bag handle to the top edge of the bag with a couple of stitches **(C)**.

Anna

Magpie Anna collects shiny things. Marbles are just about her most favourite treasures. She loves their jewel-like colours. She likes a pop of colour in her wardrobe too, hence the dusky rose ankle boots and bright owl sweater. When you have a pale Scandi complexion, and ice blond hair, a bit of vivid pink lets the world know you're coming.

You Will Need

Yarn

- **Yarn A** Tan
- **Yarn B** Cream
- **Yarn C** Dusky Rose
- **Yarn D** Aqua
- **Yarn E** Teal
- **Yarn F** Deep Fuchsia
- **Yarn G** Orange
- Scraps of black and red for eyes and mouth

You will also need

- 3mm (US 2½) straight needles
- 2.5mm (US 1½) straight needles
- 2.5mm (US 1½) double-pointed needles
- Stitch holder
- Tapestry needle
- 3 x 15mm (½in) circles of white felt
- Toy stuffing
- 4 x 6mm (¼in) buttons

Finished size

- 28cm (11in) tall

Pattern

Cast on using the Long tail cast-on (double cast-on) method (see Techniques) unless otherwise indicated. Where possible leave long tails when you cast on and cast off and use these for the sewing up.

Head

Starting at neck:

Using Yarn A and 2.5mm needles cast on 13 sts.

Row 1 (ws): Purl.

Row 2: [K1, M1] 12 times, K1. (25 sts)

Row 3: Purl.

Row 4: K3, [K1, M1] 7 times, K4, [K1, M1] 7 times, K4. (39 sts)

Rows 5–7: Stocking stitch 3 rows.

Row 8: K3, [K3, M1] 4 times, K6, [K3, M1] 4 times, K6. (47 sts)

Cut yarn.

Rows 9–31: Using Intarsia technique (see Techniques) and working in stocking stitch work Hair Chart. Start with a purl row (ws) at the bottom left hand corner of chart, read purl rows (ws) from left to right and knit rows (rs) from right to left.

For top of head continue in Yarn B.

Row 32: K8, K2tog, K4, SSK, K15, K2tog, K4, SSK, K8. (43 sts)

Row 33: Purl.

Row 34: K8, K2tog, K2, SSK, K15, K2tog, K2, SSK, K8. (39 sts)

Row 35: Purl.

Row 36: K8, K2tog, SSK, K15, K2tog, SSK, K8. (35 sts)

Cut yarn, transfer the stitches onto a stitch holder.

Pigtails

Using Yarn E and 2.5mm needles cast on 5 sts.

Row 1 (ws): Knit.

Change to Yarn B.

Row 2: Knit.

Row 3: Purl.

Row 4: K1, m1r, K3, m1l, K1. (7 sts)

Row 5: Purl.

Row 6: K1, m1r, K5, m1l, K1. (9 sts)

Rows 7–9: Stocking stitch 3 rows.

Row 10: K2 [YO, K2tog] to last st, K1.

Rows 11–13: Stocking stitch 3 rows.

Row 14: SSK, K5, K2tog. (7 sts)

Row 15: Purl.

Row 16: SSK, K3, K2tog. (5 sts)

Change to Yarn E.

Rows 17–18: Purl 2 rows.

Cast off purlwise

Body

Using Yarn A and 2.5mm needles cast on 9 sts.

Starting at neck:

Row 1 (ws): Purl.

Row 2: K1, [K1, M1] 6 times, K2. (15 sts)

Row 3: Purl.

Row 4: K2, [K1, M1] 3 times, K4, [K1, M1] 3 times, K3. (21 sts)

Row 5: Purl.

Row 6: K3, [K1, M1] 4 times, K6, [K1, M1] 4 times, K4. (29 sts)

Rows 7–9: Stocking stitch 3 rows.

Row 10: K4, [K1, M1] 6 times, K8, [K1, M1] 6 times, K5. (41 sts)

Rows 11–15: Stocking stitch 5 rows.

Row 16: K3, [K3, M1] 4 times, K8, [K3, M1] 4 times, K6. (49 sts)

Rows 17–27: Stocking stitch 11 rows.

TOP OF TIGHTS

Continue working the 49 sts on needle.

Change to Yarn D.

Rows 28–29: Knit 2 rows.

Rows 30–31: Starting with a knit row, stocking stitch 2 rows.

Change to Yarn B.

Rows 32–35: Stocking stitch 4 rows.

Change to Yarn E.

Rows 36–39: Stocking stitch 4 rows.

Change to Yarn D.

Rows 40–43: Stocking stitch 4 rows.

Cast off.

Arms

(make 2)

Using Yarn A and 2.5mm needles cast on 12 sts.

Rows 1–3: Starting with a purl row (ws), stocking stitch 3 rows.

Row 4: Cast on 3 sts using Knit Cast-on method (see Techniques), knit to end. (15 sts)

Row 5: Cast on 3 sts using Purl Cast-on method (see Techniques), purl to end. (18 sts)

Rows 6–7: Stocking stitch 2 rows.

Row 8: SSK, K14, K2tog. (16 sts)

Row 9: Purl.

Row 10: SSK, K12, K2tog. (14 sts)

Row 11: Purl.

Row 12: SSK, K10, K2tog. (12 sts)

Rows 13–47: Stocking stitch 35 rows.

Row 48: SSK, K8, K2tog. (10 sts)

Row 49: Purl.

Row 50: SSK, K6, K2tog. (8 sts)

Row 51: Purl.

Row 52: SSK, K4, K2tog. (6 sts)

Row 53: Purl.

Row 54: SSK, K2, K2tog. (4 sts)

Row 55: Purl.

Cast off.

Hair Chart

□ = Yarn A
□ = Yarn B

Legs and boots

(make 2)

Starting at sole of boot:

Using Yarn F and 2.5mm needles cast on 12 sts.

Row 1 (ws): Purl.

Row 2: K1, M1, K3, (K1, M1) 3 times, K4, M1, K1. (17 sts)

Row 3: Purl.

Row 4: (K1, M1) 2 times, K3, (K1, M1) 2 times, K2, (K1, M1) 2 times, K3, (K1, M1) 2 times, K1. (25 sts)

Row 5: Purl.

Row 6: (K2, M1) 2 times, K2, (K2, M1) 2 times, K3, (K2, M1) 2 times, K2, (K2, M1) 2 times, K2. (33 sts)

Row 7: Purl.

Row 8: (K3, M1) 2 times, K1, (K3, M1) 2 times, K4, (K3, M1) 2 times, K1, (K3, M1) 2 times, K3. (41 sts)

Row 9: Knit.

Row 10: Purl.

Change to Yarn C.

Rows 11–13: Starting with a purl row, stocking stitch 3 rows.

Row 14: K15, SSK, K7, K2tog, K15. (39 sts)

Row 15: Purl.

Row 16: K15, SSK, K5, K2tog, K15. (37 sts)

Row 17: Purl.

Row 18: K15, SSK, K3, K2tog, K15. (35 sts)

Row 19: Purl.

Row 20: K8, [K7, SSK, K1, K2tog, K7] cast off these middle 17 sts as you work them, K8. (16 sts)

Row 21: P7, P2tog, P7. (15 sts)

BOTTOM OF TIGHTS

Continue working the 15 sts on needle:

Starting with Yarn E, the tights are worked in a stripe pattern of 4 rows each of Yarn E, Yarn B and Yarn D throughout.

Rows 22–77: Stocking stitch 56 rows.

Cast off using Yarn D.

Boot cuffs

(make 2)

Starting at the top of the cuff.

Using Yarn C and 3mm needles cast on 31 sts.

Row 1 (ws): (P1, K2) to last st, P1.

Row 2: (K1, P2) to last st, K1.

Rows 3–18: Repeat last 2 rows, 8 more times.

Row 19: (P1, K2tog) to last st, P1. (21 sts)

Row 20: (K1, P1) to last st, K1.

Row 21: (P1, K1) to last st, P1.

Rows 22–28: Repeat last 2 rows, 3 more times, then repeat row 20 once more.

Cast off in pattern.

Skirt

Using Yarn C and 3mm needles cast on 73 sts.

Row 1 (ws): Knit.

Rows 2–4: Starting with a knit row, stocking stitch 3 rows.

Row 5: Knit.

Rows 6–21: Starting with a knit row, stocking stitch 16 rows.

Row 22: [K1, K2tog,] to last st, K1. (49 sts)

Row 23: Knit.

Rows 24–26: Starting with a knit row, stocking stitch 3 rows.

Row 27: Knit.

Cast off.

Sweater

Front of sweater

Using Yarn B and 3mm needles cast on 27 sts.

Row 1 (ws): Knit.

Rows 2–3: Knit 2 rows.

Rows 4–9: Starting with a knit row, stocking stitch 7 rows.

Sweater Chart A is placed in the rows that follow, using Intarsia technique (see Techniques) and worked in stocking stitch. Starting at the bottom right hand corner, read knit rows (rs) from right to left and purl rows (ws) from left to right.

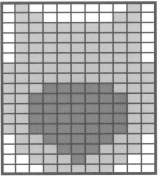

Sweater Chart A

☐ = Yarn B
▦ = Yarn D
▦ = Yarn C

Row 10: K8, work Sweater Chart A, K8.

Row 11: P8, work Sweater Chart A, P8.

Rows 12–26: Rpt the last 2 rows 7 more times, then rpt row 10 once more.

Rows 27–33: Stocking stitch 7 rows.

Cast off.

Back of sweater

Using Yarn B and 3mm needles cast on 27 sts.

Row 1 (ws): Knit.

Rows 2–3: Knit 2 rows.

Rows 4–19: Starting with a knit row, stocking stitch 16 rows.

RIGHT BUTTON PLACKET

Row 20: K15, turn. (15 sts)

Row 21: K3, P12.

Rows 22–23: Rpt last 2 rows.

Row 24: K13, YO, K2tog, turn.

Row 25: K1, Ktbl, K1, P12.

Rows 26–31: Rpt rows 20 & 21, 3 more times.

Row 32: Rpt row 24.

Row 33: Rpt row 25.

Cast off 15 sts, cut yarn.

LEFT BUTTON PLACKET

Row 1: Returning to stitches still on needle, rejoin Yarn B and pick up and knit 3 sts from BEHIND the first row of the right button placket (see Techniques, Picking Up Stitches), knit across stitches on left hand needle. (15 sts)

Row 2: P12, K3.

Row 3: Knit.

Rows 4–13: Repeat last 2 rows, 5 more times.

Row 14: P12, K3.

Cast off.

Sleeves

(make 2)

Using Yarn C and 3mm needles cast on 20 sts.

Row 1 (ws): Knit.

Starting with Yarn B, the sleeves are now worked in a stripe pattern of 2 rows each of Yarn B and Yarn D throughout.

Rows 2–23: Starting with a knit row, stocking stitch 22 rows.

Cast off.

Making Up

Doll

See Making Up Your Doll in Techniques.

Pigtails

1. With wrong sides together, fold the piece in half along the eyelet holes and then sew each side seam together.

2. Stitch in place on either side of Anna's head **(A)**.

Clothing

Sweater

1. Using Sweater Chart B, work the owl's eyes, beak and feet in Duplicate stitch (also known as Swiss darning, see Techniques).

2. Block all the pieces of the sweater before making up.

3. Now sew the buttons into place on the centre of each eye **(B)** and on the back of the sweater, matching them up with the button holes **(C)**.

4. Sew up shoulder seams leaving a big enough gap to fit around neck. Sew sleeves to front and back pieces lining up centre of sleeves to shoulder seams. Sew up sleeve and sweater edge seams.

Skirt

1. Block skirt befire making up.

2. Starting at the hem sew the edges of the skirt together, creating a side seam.

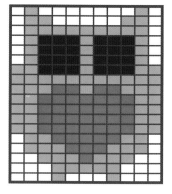

Sweater Chart B

☐ = Yarn B ▪ = Yarn C

▪ = Yarn D ▪ = Yarn E

▪ = Yarn G

(A)

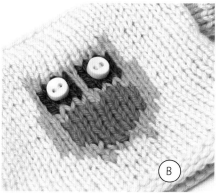

(B)

(C)

Pippa

A creative little soul, Pippa is never happier than when she's making something lovely. This week it's a beautiful scrapbook using pretty washi tape. Last week she learnt how to knit little flowers. She became an unstoppable flower-knitting machine, and her mummy had to suggest scrapbooking before Pippa's entire wardrobe went 'floral'.

You Will Need

Yarn

- **Yarn A** Cream
- **Yarn B** Camel
- **Yarn C** Nectarine
- **Yarn D** Sage Green
- Scraps of black and red for eyes and mouth

Finished size

- 28cm (11in) tall

You will also need

- 3mm (US 2½) straight needles
- 2.5mm (US 1½) straight needles
- 2.5mm (US 1½) double-pointed needles
- Stitch holder
- Tapestry needle
- 3 x 15mm (½in) circles of white felt
- Toy stuffing
- 8 x 6mm (¼in) buttons

Pattern

Cast on using the Long-tail (double cast on) method (see Techniques) unless otherwise indicated. Where possible leave long tails when you cast on and cast off and use these for the sewing up.

Head

Starting at neck:

Using Yarn A and 2.5mm needles cast on 13 sts.

Row 1 (ws): Purl.

Row 2: [K1, M1] 12 times, K1. (25 sts)

Row 3: Purl.

Row 4: K3, [K1, M1] 7 times, K4, [K1, M1] 7 times, K4. (39 sts)

Rows 5–7: Stocking stitch 3 rows.

Row 8: K3, [K3, M1] 4 times, K6, [K3, M1] 4 times, K6. (47 sts)

Cut yarn.

Rows 9–31: Using Intarsia technique (see Techniques) and working in stocking stitch work Hair Chart. Start with a purl row (ws) at the bottom left hand corner of chart, read purl rows (ws) from left to right and knit rows (rs) from right to left.

For top of head continue in Yarn B.

Row 32: K8, K2tog, K4, SSK, K15, K2tog, K4, SSK, K8. (43 sts)

Row 33: Purl.

Row 34: K8, K2tog, K2, SSK, K15, K2tog, K2, SSK, K8. (39 sts)

Row 35: Purl.

Row 36: K8, K2tog, SSK, K15, K2tog, SSK, K8. (35 sts)

Cut yarn, transfer the stitches onto a stitch holder.

Right pigtail

Using Yarn B and 2.5mm needles cast on 13 sts.

Row 1 (ws): Purl.

Row 2: K1, *[Kfb] 2 times, K4; rep from * once more. (17 sts)

Rows 3–5: Stocking stitch 3 rows.

Row 6: K9, K2tog, SSK, K4. (15 sts)

Row 7: Purl.

Row 8: K1, [K2tog, SSK, K3] 2 times. (11 sts)

Row 9: Purl.

Row 10: K5, K2tog, SSK, K2. (9 sts)

Row 11: P1, SSP, P2tog, P4. (7 sts)

Row 12: K2tog, K3tog, SSK. (3 sts)

Row 13: Purl.

Cut yarn leaving a long tail, thread tail through the stitches left on needle and draw up.

Left pigtail

Using Yarn B and 2.5mm needles cast on 13 sts.

Row 1 (ws): Purl.

Row 2: *K4, [Kfb] 2 times; rep from * once more, K1. (17 sts)

Rows 3–5: Stocking stitch 3 rows.

Row 6: K4, K2tog, SSK, K9. (15 sts)

Row 7: Purl.

Row 8: [K3, K2tog, SSK] 2 times, K1. (11 sts)

Row 9: Purl.

Row 10: K2, K2tog, SSK, K5. (9 sts)

Row 11: P4, SSP, P2tog, P1. (7 sts)

Row 12: K2tog, Sl1, SSK, PSSO, SSK. (3 sts)

Row 13: Purl.

Cut yarn leaving a long tail, thread tail through the stitches left on needle and draw up.

Head band

Band

Using Yarn D and 3mm needles cast on 47 sts.

Row 1 (ws): [P1, K1] to last st, P1.

Cast off.

Flowers

(make 3)

Using Yarn A and 2.5mm needles cast on 12 sts.

Row 1 (ws): Knit.

Row 2: [K2tog] to end.

Cut yarn leaving a long tail, thread tail through the stitches left on needle and draw up.

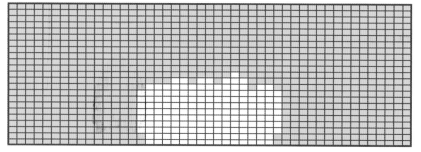

Hair Chart

☐ = Yarn A
☐ = Yarn B

Body

Using Yarn A and 2.5mm needles cast on 9 sts.

Starting at neck:

Row 1 (ws): Purl.

Row 2: K1, [K1, M1] 6 times, K2. (15 sts)

Row 3: Purl.

Row 4: K2, [K1, M1] 3 times, K4, [K1, M1] 3 times, K3. (21 sts)

Row 5: Purl.

Row 6: K3, [K1, M1] 4 times, K6, [K1, M1] 4 times, K4. (29 sts)

Rows 7–9: Stocking stitch 3 rows.

Row 10: K4, [K1, M1] 6 times, K8, [K1, M1] 6 times, K5. (41 sts)

Rows 11–15: Stocking stitch 5 rows.

Row 16: K3, [K3, M1] 4 times, K8, [K3, M1] 4 times, K6. (49 sts)

Rows 17–27: Stocking stitch 11 rows.

KNICKERS

Continue working the 49 sts on needle.

Change to Yarn D.

Rows 28–29: Knit 2 rows.

Starting with Yarn C, the knickers are now worked in a stripe pattern of 2 rows Yarn C and 2 rows Yarn A throughout.

Rows 30–43: Starting with a knit row, stocking stitch 14 rows.

Cast off using Yarn A.

Arms

(make 2)

Using Yarn A and 2.5mm needles cast on 12 sts.

Rows 1–3: Starting with a purl row (ws), stocking stitch 3 rows.

Row 4: Cast on 3 sts using knit cast-on method (see Techniques section), knit to end. (15 sts)

Row 5: Cast on 3 sts using purl cast-on method (see Techniques section), purl to end. (18 sts)

Rows 6–7: Stocking stitch 2 rows.

Row 8: SSK, K14, K2tog. (16 sts)

Row 9: Purl.

Row 10: SSK, K12, K2tog. (14 sts)

Row 11: Purl.

Row 12: SSK, K10, K2tog. (12 sts)

Rows 13–47: Stocking stitch 35 rows.

Row 48: SSK, K8, K2tog. (10 sts)

Row 49: Purl.

Row 50: SSK, K6, K2tog. (8 sts)

Row 51: Purl.

Row 52: SSK, K4, K2tog. (6 sts)

Row 53: Purl.

Row 54: SSK, K2, K2tog. (4 sts)

Row 55: Purl.

Cast off.

Legs

(make 2)

Starting at top of leg:

Using Yarn A and 2.5mm needles cast on 16 sts.

Rows 1–55: Starting with a purl row (ws), stocking stitch 55 rows.

TOP OF FOOT

Row 56: Cast off 5 sts, knit to end. (11 sts)

Row 57: Cast off 5 sts pw, purl to end. (6 sts)

Rows 58–75: Stocking stitch 18 rows.

Cast off row: SSK, K2, K2tog (cast off all sts as you work them).

T-bar shoes

(make 2)

Using Yarn C and 2.5mm needles cast on 12 sts.

Row 1 (ws): Purl.

Row 2: K1, M1, K3, [K1, M1] 3 times, K4, M1, K1. (17 sts)

Row 3: Purl.

Row 4: [K1, M1] 2 times, K3, [K1, M1] 2 times, K2, [K1, M1] 2 times, K3, [K1, M1] 2 times, K1. (25 sts)

Row 5: Purl.

Row 6: [K2, M1] 2 times, K2, [K2, M1] 2 times, K3, [K2, M1] 2 times, K2, [K2, M1] 2 times, K2. (33 sts)

Row 7: Purl.

Row 8: [K3, M1] 2 times, K1, [K3, M1] 2 times, K4, [K3, M1] 2 times, K1, [K3, M1] 2 times, K3. (41 sts)

Rows 9–13: Stocking stitch 5 rows.

Row 14: K15, SSK, K7, K2tog, K15. (39 sts)

Row 15: Purl.

Row 16: K15, SSK, K5, K2tog, K15. (37 sts)

Row 17: Purl.

Row 18: Cast off 15 sts, SSK, K3, K2tog, knit to end. (20 sts)

Row 19: Cast off 15 sts pw, purl to end. (5 sts)

Row 20: SSK, K1, K2tog.

Row 21: K1, P1, K1.

Row 22: Knit.

Rows 23–29: Rpt last 2 rows, 3 more times, then rpt row 21 once more.

Row 30: K1, sl1 pw with yarn at back, K1.

Row 31: K1, sl1 pw with yarn at front, K1.

Cast off.

Shoe straps

(make 2)

Using Yarn C and 2.5mm needles cast on 10 sts.

Row 1 (ws): K7, P3.

Row 2: K3, turn.

Row 3: P3.

Cast off knitwise.

Dress

Front of dress

Using Yarn D and 3mm needles cast on 37 sts.

Row 1 (ws): [K1, P1] to last st, K1.

Rows 2–3: Rpt last row, 2 more times.

Rows 4–37: Starting with a knit row, stocking stitch 34 rows.

Row 38: [K1, K2tog] to last st, K1. (25 sts)

Row 39: [K1, P1] to last st, K1.

Row 40: P2tog, [K1, P1] to last 3 sts, K1, SSP. (23 sts)

Row 41: [P1, K1] to last st, P1.

Row 42: SSK, [P1, K1] to last 3 sts, P1, K2tog. (21 sts)

Row 43: [K1, P1] to last st, K1.

Row 44: P2tog, [K1, P1] to last 3 sts, K1, SSP. (19 sts)

Row 45: [P1, K1] to last st, P1.

Rows 46–55: Rpt last row, 10 more times.

Cast off in pattern.

Back of dress

Using Yarn D and 3mm needles cast on 37 sts.

Row 1 (ws): [K1, P1] to last st, K1.

Rows 2–3: Rpt last row, 2 more times.

Rows 4–37: Starting with a knit row, stocking stitch 34 rows.

Row 38: [K1, K2tog] to last st, K1. (25 sts)

Row 39: [K1, P1] to last st, K1.

RIGHT BUTTON PLACKET

Row 40: P2tog, [K1, P1] 6 times, turn. (13 sts)

Row 41: [P1, K1] to last st, P1.

Row 42: SSK, [P1, K1] 5 times, P1, turn. (12 sts)

Row 43: [P1, K1] to end.

Row 44: P2tog, [K1, P1] 5 times, turn. (11 sts)

Row 45: [P1, K1] to last st, P1.

Row 46: [P1, K1] 4 times, P1, YO, P2tog, turn.

Row 47: P1, Ktbl, [P1, K1] to last st, P1.

Row 48: [P1, K1] to last st, P1, turn.

Row 49: [P1, K1] to last st, P1.

Rows 50–53: Rpt last 2 rows, 2 more times.

Row 54: [P1, K1] 4 times, P1, YO, P2tog, turn.

Row 55: P1, Ktbl, [P1, K1] to last st, P1.

Cast off 11 sts in pattern, cut yarn.

LEFT BUTTON PLACKET

Row 1: Returning to stitches still on needle, rejoin Yarn C and pick up and knit 3 sts from behind the first row of right button placket (see Techniques, Picking Up Stitches), [K1, P1] across stitches on left-hand needle to last 3 sts, K1, SSP. (13 sts)

Row 2 (ws): [P1, K1] to last st, P1.

Row 3: [P1, K1] to last 3 sts, P1, K2tog. (12 sts)

Row 4: [K1, P1] to end.

Row 5: [P1, K1] to last 2 sts, SSP. (11 sts)

Row 6: [P1, K1] to last st, P1.

Rows 7–16: Rpt last row, 10 more times.

Cast off in pattern.

Flower

Using Yarn A and 2.5mm needles cast on 31 sts.

FIRST PETAL

Row 1 (ws): Slip 1 purlwise, P5, turn.

Row 2: K5, turn.

Row 3: P5, turn.

Row 4: K6, turn.

Row 5: [P2tog] 3 times.

REMAINING PETALS

Rpt rows 1–5, four more times until 1 st remains, P1.

Row 6: K1, [slip 2 together knitwise, K1, PSSO] to end.

Cut yarn leaving a long tail. Using a tapestry needle thread the tail through the stitches left on needle and draw up.

Cardigan

Right front of cardigan

Using Yarn C and 3mm needles cast on 15 sts.

Row 1 (ws): [K1, P1] to last st, K1.

Rows 2–3: Rpt last row, 2 more times.

Row 4: K1, P1, knit to end.

Row 5: Purl to last 3 sts, K1, P1, K1.

Rows 6–21: Rpt last 2 rows, 8 more times.

Row 22: K1, P1, K1, SSSK, knit to end. (13 sts)

Row 23: Rpt row 5.

Row 24: K1, P1, K1, SSSK, knit to end. (11 sts)

Row 25: Rpt row 5.

Row 26: K1, P1, K1, SSSK, knit to end. (9 sts)

Row 27: Rpt row 5.

Row 28: K1, P1, K1, SSSK, knit to end. (7 sts)

Row 29: Rpt row 5.

Cast off.

Left front of cardigan

Using Yarn C and 3mm needles cast on 15 sts.

Row 1 (ws): [K1, P1] to last st, K1.

Row 2: [K1, P1] to last 3 sts, K1, YO, K2tog.

Row 3: Rpt row 1.

Row 4: Knit to last 2 sts, P1, K1.

Row 5: K1, P1, K1, purl to end.

Rows 6–10: Rpt last 2 rows, 2 more times, then rpt row 4 once more.

Row 11: K1, YO, K2tog, purl to end.

Row 12: Knit to last 2 sts, P1, K1.

Row 13: K1, P1, K1, purl to end.

Rows 14–19: Rpt last 2 rows, 3 more times.

Row 20: Knit to last 2 sts, YO, K2tog.

Row 21: K1, P1, K1, purl to end.

Row 22: K9, K3tog, K1, P1, K1. (13 sts)

Row 23: Rpt row 5.

Row 24: K7, K3tog, K1, P1, K1. (11 sts)

Row 25: Rpt row 5.

Row 26: K5, K3tog, K1, P1, K1. (9 sts)

Row 27: Rpt row 5.

Row 28: K3, K3tog, K1, P1, K1. (7 sts)

Row 29: Rpt row 5.

Cast off.

Back of cardigan

Using Yarn C and 3mm needles cast on 27 sts.

Row 1 (ws): [K1, P1] to last st, K1.

Rows 2–3: Rpt last row, 2 more times.

Rows 4–26: Stocking stitch 23 rows.

Row 27: P4, [K1, P1] to last 3 sts, P3.

Row 28: K5, [P1, K1] to last 4 sts, K4.

Row 29: P4, [K1, P1] to last 3 sts, P3.

Cast off.

Sleeves of cardigan

(make 2)

Using Yarn C and 3mm needles cast on 15 sts.

Row 1 (ws): [K1, P1] to last st, K1.

Rows 2–3: Rpt last row, 2 more times.

Row 4: K1, [K1, Kfb] 6 times, K2. (21 sts)

Rows 5–25: Starting with a purl row, stocking stitch 21 rows.

Cast off.

Making Up

Doll

See Making Up Your Doll in Techniques.

Pigtails

1. Start by folding each side of the pigtail to the back along the middle of both sets of decreases (**A**).

2. Sew the edges together forming a slightly off centre back seam (**B**).

3. Press flat and do not stuff. Sewing through the cast on edges of pigtails, attach them to each side of the head, making sure the back seam is facing towards the back of the completed head then bury loose ends in head (**C**).

Clothing

Dress

1. Block all the pieces of the dress before making up.

2. Start by sewing the buttons into place on the back of the dress, matching them up with the button holes (**D**).

3. Sew up the shoulder seams, make sure you leave a big enough gap to fit around Pippa's neck.

4. Sew up the edge seams, leaving a 2.5cm (1in) gap at the top for the arm holes.

5. Join the first and last petals of the flower together at the 'cast on' edge with a small stitch.

6. Sew onto the front of the dress then add a contrasting button in the centre of the flower to finish (**E**)

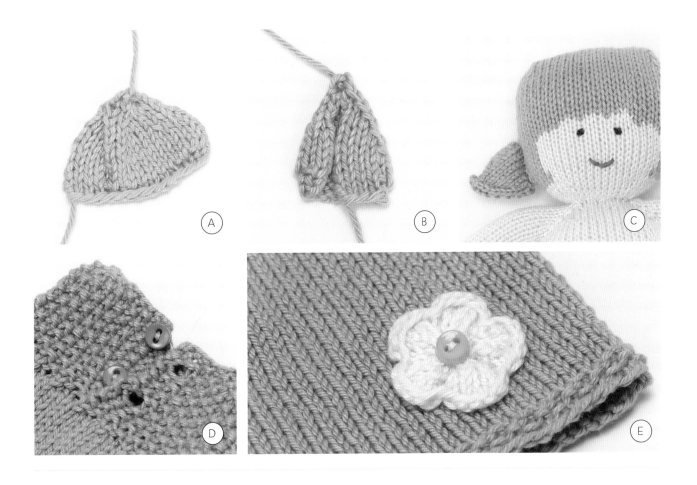

Cardigan

1. Block all the pieces of the cardigan before making up.

2. Start by sewing up the shoulder seams, then sew the sleeves to the front and back pieces, lining up the centre of the sleeves to the shoulder seams.

3. Sew up the sleeve and body edge seams.

4. Sew the buttons into place on the right button band, matching them up with the button holes (**F**).

5. Finally add the contrast stitching detail using a running stitch. Starting at the right hand side seam, work along the bottom front edge then up towards the neck, continuing all the way around until you reach your starting point (**F**). Weave ends in along the side seam.

Head band

Sew the ends of the band together. Form the flowers by sewing the first and last cast on stitches together then knot both tail ends together to secure. Using a sewing needle and thread attach each flower to the band. To finish work a French knot (see Techniques) in contrasting yarn in the centre of each flower (**G**).

(F)

(G)

Jane

When it comes to cakes and cafés, Jane is the queen. She's been to all the ones near where she lives because mummy is always 'gasping for a coffee' after a busy morning shopping. In her sophisticated beret, cardi and buttoned skirt, she'll settle down happily with a babycino and an enormous double-choc muffin.

You Will Need

Yarn

- **Yarn A** Beige
- **Yarn B** Chestnut
- **Yarn C** Cream
- **Yarn D** Navy
- **Yarn E** Pale Denim
- **Yarn F** Mustard
- Scraps of black and red for eyes, mouth and details

Finished size

- 28cm (11in) tall

You will also need

- 3mm (US 2½) straight needles
- 2.5mm (US 1½) straight needles
- 2.5mm (US 1½) double-pointed needles
- Stitch holder
- Tapestry needle
- 3 x 15mm (½in) circles of white felt
- Toy stuffing
- 6 x 6mm (¼in) buttons
- 2 short lengths of 5mm wide ribbon

Pattern

Cast on using the Long-tail (double cast on) method (see Techniques) unless otherwise indicated. Where possible leave long tails when you cast on and cast off and use these for the sewing up.

Head

Starting at neck:

Using Yarn A and 2.5mm needles cast on 13 sts.

Row 1 (ws): Purl.

Row 2: [K1, M1] 12 times, K1. (25 sts)

Row 3: Purl.

Row 4: K3, [K1, M1] 7 times, K4, [K1, M1] 7 times, K4. (39 sts)

Rows 5–7: Stocking stitch 3 rows.

Row 8: K3, [K3, M1] 4 times, K6, [K3, M1] 4 times, K6. (47 sts)

Cut yarn.

Rows 9–31: Using Intarsia technique (see Techniques) and working in stocking stitch work Hair Chart. Start with a purl row (ws) at the bottom left hand corner of chart, read purl rows (ws) from left to right and knit rows (rs) from right to left.

For top of head continue in Yarn B.

Row 32: K8, K2tog, K4, SSK, K15, K2tog, K4, SSK, K8. (43 sts)

Row 33: Purl.

Row 34: K8, K2tog, K2, SSK, K15, K2tog, K2, SSK, K8 (39 sts)

Row 35: Purl.

Row 36: K8, K2tog, SSK, K15, K2tog, SSK, K8. (35 sts)

Cut yarn, transfer the stitches onto a stitch holder.

Pigtails

(make 2)

Using 2.5mm dpns and Yarn B, cast on 5 sts and make an i-cord of 22 rows (see Techniques section).

Body

T-SHIRT

Using Yarn C and 2.5mm needles cast on 9 sts.

Starting at neck:

Row 1 (ws): Purl.

Row 2: K1, [K1, M1] 6 times, K2. (15 sts)

Row 3: Purl.

The T-shirt is now worked in a stripe pattern of 2 rows Yarn D and 4 rows Yarn C, starting with Yarn D.

Row 4: K2, [K1, M1] 3 times, K4, [K1, M1] 3 times, K3 (21 sts)

Row 5: Purl.

Row 6: K3, [K1, M1] 4 times, K6, [K1, M1] 4 times, K4. (29 sts)

Rows 7–9: Stocking stitch 3 rows.

Row 10: K4, [K1, M1] 6 times, K8, [K1, M1] 6 times, K5. (41 sts)

Rows 11–15: Stocking stitch 5 rows.

Row 16: K3, [K3, M1] 4 times, K8, [K3, M1] 4 times, K6. (49 sts)

Rows 17–27: Stocking stitch 11 rows.

TOP OF LEGGINGS

Continue working the 49 sts on needle.

Change to Yarn E.

Rows 28–29: Knit 2 rows.

Rows 30–43: Starting with a knit row, stocking stitch 14 rows.

Cast off.

Arms

(make 2)

Using Yarn A and 2.5mm needles cast on 12 sts.

Rows 1–3: Starting with a purl row (ws), stocking stitch 3 rows.

Row 4: Cast on 3 sts using knit cast-on method (see Techniques section), knit to end. (15 sts)

Row 5: Cast on 3 sts using purl cast-on method (see Techniques section), purl to end. (18 sts)

Rows 6–7: Stocking stitch 2 rows.

Row 8: SSK, K14, K2tog. (16 sts)

Row 9: Purl.

Row 10: SSK, K12, K2tog. (14 sts)

Row 11: Purl.

Row 12: SSK, K10, K2tog. (12 sts)

SLEEVES

Continue working the 12 sts on needle.

The sleeves are worked in a stripe pattern of 2 rows Yarn D and 4 rows Yarn C throughout, starting with Yarn D.

Rows 13–14: Purl 2 rows.

Rows 15–47: Starting with a purl row, stocking stitch 33 rows.

Row 48: SSK, K8, K2tog. (10 sts)

Row 49: Purl.

Row 50: SSK, K6, K2tog. (8 sts)

Row 51: Purl.

Row 52: SSK, K4, K2tog. (6 sts)

Row 53: Purl.

Row 54: SSK, K2, K2tog. (4 sts)

Row 55: Purl.

Cast off.

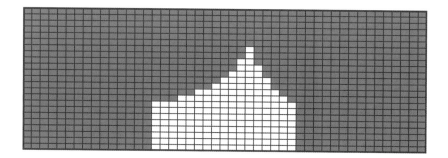

Hair Chart

☐ = Yarn A
■ = Yarn B

Legs and sneakers

(make 2)

Starting at base of sneaker:

Using Yarn E and 2.5mm needles cast on 12 sts.

Row 1 (ws): Purl

Row 2: K1, M1, K3, (K1, M1) 3 times, K4, M1, K1. (17 sts)

Row 3: Purl.

Row 4: (K1, M1) 2 times, K3, (K1, M1) 2 times, K2, (K1, M1)2 times, K3, (K1, M1) 2 times, K1. (25 sts)

Row 5: Purl.

Row 6: (K2, M1) 2 times, K2, (K2, M1) 2 times, K3, (K2, M1) 2 times, K2, (K2, M1) 2 times, K2. (33 sts)

Row 7: Purl.

Change to Yarn C

Row 8: (K3, M1) 2 times, K1, (K3, M1) 2 times, K4, (K3, M1) 2 times, K1, (K3, M1) 2 times, K3. (41 sts)

Row 9: Knit.

Row 10: Purl.

The next 8 rows use intarsia technique (see Techniques section) for changing yarns:

(D) = Use Yarn D (C) = Use Yarn C.

Row 11: (D) P14, (C) P13, (D) P14.

Row 12: (D) K14, (C) K13, (D) K14.

Row 13: (D) P14, (C) P13, (D) P14.

Row 14: (D) K14, (C) K1, SSK, K7, K2tog, K1, (D) K14. (39 sts)

Row 15: (D) P14, (C) P11, (D) P14.

Row 16: (D) K14, (C) K1, SSK, K5, K2tog, K1, (D) K14. (37 sts)

Row 17: (D) P14, (C) P9, (D) P14.

Row 18: (D) K7, (C) K8, SSK, K3, K2tog, K8, (D) K7. (35 sts)

Change to Yarn C.

Row 19: Purl.

Row 20: P8, [K7, SSK, K1, K2tog, K7] cast off these middle 17 sts as you work them, P to end. (16 sts)

LEGS AND LEGGINGS

Continue working the 16 sts on needle:

Change to Yarn A.

Row 21: P7, P2tog, P7. (15 sts)

Rows 22–31: Stocking stitch 10 rows.

Change to Yarn D.

Row 32–33: Knit 2 rows.

Change to Yarn E.

Row 34–35: Starting with a knit row, stocking stitch 2 rows

Change to Yarn D.

Row 36–37: Stocking stitch 2 rows.

Rows 38–69: Rpt last 4 rows 8 more times.

Change to Yarn E.

Row 70–77: Stocking stitch 8 rows.

Cast off.

Skirt

Using Yarn E and 3mm needles cast on 57 sts.

Row 1 (ws): Knit.

Row 2: Knit.

Row 3: P27, K3, P27.

Row 4: Knit.

Rows 5–14: Rpt last 2 rows 5 more times.

Row 15: P15, K8, P4, K3, P4, K8, P15.

Row 16: Knit.

Rows 17–22: Rpt last 2 rows 3 more times.

Row 23: P17, K6, P4, K3, P4, K6, P17.

Row 24: Knit.

Row 25: P18, K5, P4, K3, P4, K5, P18.

Row 26: Knit.

Row 27: P19, K4, P4, K3, P4, K4, P19.

Row 28: Knit.

Row 29: P19, K4, P4, K3, P4, K4, P19.

Row 30: [K2, K2tog,] to last st, K1. (43 sts)

Row 31: K3, [P1, K6] 2 times, P1, K7, [P1, K6] 2 times, P1, K3.

Row 32: Knit.

Row 33: K3, [P1, K6] 2 times, P1, K7, [P1, K6] 2 times, P1, K3.

Cast off.

Cardigan

The cardigan is worked in one piece from the top down.

Using Yarn F and 3mm needles cast on 33 sts.

Row 1 (ws): Knit.

Row 2: K1, YO, K2tog, knit to end.

Row 3: K3, purl to last 3 sts, K3.

Row 4: K3, [Kfb, K1] to last 4 sts, Kfb, K3. (47 sts)

Row 5: K3, purl to last 3 sts, K3.

Rows 6–7: Knit 2 rows.

Row 8: K3, [Kfb, K2] to last 5 sts, Kfb, K4. (61 sts)

Row 9: K3, purl to last 3 sts, K3.

Rows 10–11: Knit 2 rows.

Row 12: K3, [Kfb, K3] to last 2 sts, K2. (75 sts)

Row 13: K3, purl to last 3 sts, K3.

Rows 14–15: Knit 2 rows.

Row 16: K3, [Kfb, K4] to last 2 sts, K2. (89 sts)

Row 17: K3, purl to last 3 sts, K3.

Row 18: K14, cast off 18 sts, K25, cast off 18 sts, K14. (53 sts)

Row 19: K3, P10, P2fb, P23, P2fb, P10, K3. (57 sts)

Row 20: Knit.

Row 21: K3, purl to last 3 sts, K3.

Rows 22–31: Rpt last 2 rows 5 more times.

Rows 32–35: Knit 4 rows.

Cast off.

Scottie dog bag

Bag

Using Yarn D and 2.5mm needles cast on 24 sts.

Row 1 (ws): Purl.

Row 2: [K1, M1, K10, M1, K1] 2 times. (28 sts)

Row 3: Purl.

Bag Chart A is placed in the following rows using Intarsia technique (see Techniques) and worked in stocking stitch. Starting at the bottom right hand corner, read knit rows (rs) from right to left and purl rows (ws) from left to right.

Row 4: K2, work Bag Chart A, K15.

Row 5: P15, work Bag Chart A, P2.

Rows 6–15: Rpt the last 2 rows 5 more times.

Rows 16–17: Stocking stitch 2 rows.

Row 18: K7, YO, K2tog, knit to end.

Row 19: Purl.

Cast off.

Handle

Using Yarn D and 3mm needles cast on 60 sts.

Row 1 (ws): Knit and cast off all stitches.

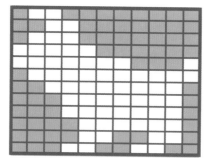

Bag Chart A

☐ = Yarn C

■ = Yarn D

Beret

Using Yarn E and 3mm needles cast on 36 sts.

Row 1 (ws): Knit.

Rows 2–3: Knit 2 rows.

Row 4: Kfb to end. (72 sts)

Rows 5–13: Stocking stitch 9 rows.

Row 14: [K5, sl2tog kw, K1, PSSO, K4] to end. (60 sts)

Row 15: Purl.

Row 16: [K4, sl2tog kw, K1, PSSO, K3] to end. (48 sts)

Row 17: Purl.

Row 18: [K3, sl2tog kw, K1, PSSO, K2] to end. (36 sts)

Row 19: Purl.

Row 20: [K2, sl2tog kw, K1, PSSO, K1] to end. (24 sts)

Row 21: Purl.

Row 22: [K1, sl2tog kw, K1, PSSO] to end. (12 sts)

Row 23: Purl.

Row 24: K2tog to end. (6 sts)

Row 25: Purl.

Row 26: K2tog to end. (3 sts)

Transfer the stitches on to a dpn and work an i-cord of 2 rows (see Techniques).

Cut yarn leaving a long tail, using a tapestry needle thread tail through the stitches left on needle and draw up.

Making Up

Doll

See Making Up Your Doll in Techniques.

Pigtails

Bend the I-cord in half forming a loop and tie the cast on and off tail ends together to secure. Sew these ends to the side of the completed head with a few stitches, then finish with a small piece of ribbon tied in a bow **(A)**.

Clothing & Accessories

Skirt

1. Block the skirt piece before making up.

2. Start by sewing the buttons down the centre front of the skirt. Sew the back seam together.

Cardigan

1. Block the cardigan bfore making up.

2. then sew the button in place on the front button band, matching it up with the button hole **(B)**.

Bag

1. Using bag chart B, work the collar detail in Duplicate stitch (also known as Swiss darning, see Techniques).

2. Block the bag pieces before you make up.

3. Start by sewing the side and bottom edges of the bag together.

4. Then attach each end of the bag handle to the top edge of the bag with a couple of stitches.

5. Finally, sew the button into place on the inside back of bag, matching it up with the button hole **(C)**.

Beret

Sew the side edges of beret together, then block.

Tip

TO BLOCK THE BERET STRETCH IT OVER A SMALL ROUND DISC OR LID, ABOUT 6.5CM (2^1/$_2$IN) IN DIAMETER, THEN SPRAY WITH WATER AND LEAVE TO DRY.

B

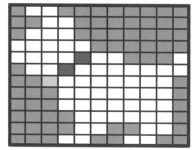

Bag Chart B

☐ = Yarn C ▨ = Yarn D
▨ = Yarn F ■ = Scrap of red

C

Alice

When her friend asked her to help re-pot some plants, Alice put on her favourite striped hoodie and got stuck in. She'd never gardened before and in retrospect the pristine white socks and pale yellow dress might have been a mistake – she hadn't realised there would be quite so much compost involved. Still, socks can always be washed... by mummy.

You Will Need

Yarn

- **Yarn A** Tan
- **Yarn B** Brown
- **Yarn C** Pale Yellow
- **Yarn D** Pink
- **Yarn E** Red
- **Yarn F** White
- Scraps of black and red for eyes and mouth

Finished size

- 28cm (11in) tall

You will also need

- 3mm (US 2½) straight needles
- 2.5mm (US 1½) straight needles
- 2.5mm (US 1½) double-pointed needles
- Stitch holder
- Tapestry needle
- 2 x 15mm (½in) circles of white felt
- Toy stuffing
- 7 x 6mm (¼in) buttons

Pattern

Cast on using the Long-tail (double cast on) method (see Techniques) unless otherwise indicated. Where possible leave long tails when you cast on and cast off and use these for the sewing up.

Head

Starting at neck:

Using Yarn A and 2.5mm needles cast on 13 sts.

Row 1 (ws): Purl.

Row 2: [K1, M1] 12 times, K1. (25 sts)

Row 3: Purl.

Row 4: K3, [K1, M1] 7 times, K4, [K1, M1] 7 times, K4. (39 sts)

Rows 5–7: Stocking stitch 3 rows.

Row 8: K3, [K3, M1] 4 times, K6, [K3, M1] 4 times, K6. (47 sts)

Cut yarn.

Rows 9–31: Using Intarsia technique (see Techniques) and working in stocking stitch work Hair Chart. Start with a purl row (ws) at the bottom left hand corner of chart, read purl rows (ws) from left to right and knit rows (rs) from right to left.

For top of head continue in Yarn B.

Row 32: K8, K2tog, K4, SSK, K15, K2tog, K4, SSK, K8. (43 sts)

Row 33: Purl.

Row 34: K8, K2tog, K2, SSK, K15, K2tog, K2, SSK, K8. (39 sts)

Row 35: Purl.

Row 36: K8, K2tog, SSK, K15, K2tog, SSK, K8. (35 sts)

Cut yarn, transfer the stitches onto a stitch holder.

Hair bob

Using Yarn B and 2.5mm needles cast on 29 sts.

Rows 1–3: Starting with a purl row (ws), stocking stitch 3 rows.

Cut yarn and transfer the stitches onto a second stitch holder.

Body

T-SHIRT

Using Yarn F and 2.5mm needles cast on 9 sts.

Starting at neck:

Row 1 (ws): Purl.

Row 2: K1, [K1, M1] 6 times, K2. (15 sts)

Row 3: Purl.

Row 4: K2, [K1, M1] 3 times, K4, [K1, M1] 3 times, K3. (21 sts)

Row 5: Purl.

Row 6: K3, [K1, M1] 4 times, K6, [K1, M1] 4 times, K4. (29 sts)

Rows 7–9: Stocking stitch 3 rows.

Row 10: K4, [K1, M1] 6 times, K8, [K1, M1] 6 times, K5. (41 sts)

Rows 11–15: Stocking stitch 5 rows.

Row 16: K3, [K3, M1] 4 times, K8, [K3, M1] 4 times, K6. (49 sts)

Rows 17–26: Stocking stitch 10 rows.

Rows 27: Knit.

KNICKERS

Continue working the 49 sts on needle.

Change to Yarn D

Rows 28–43: Starting with a knit row, stocking stitch 16 rows.

Cast off.

Arms

(make 2)

Using Yarn A and 2.5mm needles cast on 12 sts.

Rows 1–3: Starting with a purl row (ws), stocking stitch 3 rows.

Row 4: Cast on 3 sts using Knit Cast-on method (see Techniques), knit to end. (15 sts)

Row 5: Cast on 3 sts using Purl Cast-on method (see Techniques), purl to end. (18 sts)

Rows 6–7: Stocking stitch 2 rows.

Row 8: SSK, K14, K2tog. (16 sts)

Row 9: Purl.

Row 10: SSK, K12, K2tog. (14 sts)

Row 11: Purl.

Row 12: SSK, K10, K2tog. (12 sts)

Rows 13–31: Stocking stitch 19 rows.

SLEEVES

Continue working the 12 sts on needle.

Change to Yarn F.

Rows 32–33: Knit 2 rows.

Rows 34–47: Starting with a knit row, stocking stitch 14 rows.

Row 48: SSK, K8, K2tog. (10 sts)

Row 49: Purl.

Row 50: SSK, K6, K2tog. (8 sts)

Row 51: Purl.

Row 52: SSK, K4, K2tog. (6 sts)

Row 53: Purl.

Row 54: SSK, K2, K2tog. (4 sts)

Row 55: Purl.

Cast off.

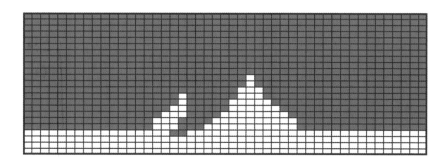

Hair Chart

□ = Yarn A

■ = Yarn B

Legs

(make 2)

Starting at top of leg:

Using Yarn A and 2.5mm needles cast on 16 sts.

Rows 1–33: Starting with a purl row (ws), stocking stitch 33 rows.

SOCKS

Change to Yarn F.

Rows 34–37: Knit 4 rows.

Rows 38–39: Starting with knit row, stocking stitch 2 rows.

Change to Yarn C.

Rows 40–41: Stocking stitch 2 rows.

Change to Yarn F.

Rows 42–55: Stocking stitch 14 rows.

TOP OF FOOT

Row 56: Cast off 5 sts, knit to end. (11 sts)

Row 57: Cast off 5 sts pw, purl to end. (6 sts)

Rows 58–75: Stocking stitch 18 rows.

Cast off row: SSK, K2, K2tog (cast off all sts as you work them).

T-bar shoes

(make 2)

Using Yarn C and 2.5mm needles cast on 12 sts.

Row 1 (ws): Purl.

Row 2: K1, M1, K3, [K1, M1] 3 times, K4, M1, K1. (17 sts)

Row 3: Purl.

Row 4: [K1, M1] 2 times, K3, [K1, M1] 2 times, K2, [K1, M1] 2 times, K3, [K1, M1] 2 times, K1. (25 sts)

Row 5: Purl.

Row 6: [K2, M1] 2 times, K2, [K2, M1] 2 times, K3, [K2, M1] 2 times, K2, [K2, M1] 2 times, K2. (33 sts)

Row 7: Purl.

Row 8: [K3, M1] 2 times, K1, [K3, M1] 2 times, K4, [K3, M1] 2 times, K1, [K3, M1] 2 times, K3. (41 sts)

Rows 9–13: Stocking stitch 5 rows.

Row 14: K15, SSK, K7, K2tog, K15. (39 sts)

Row 15: Purl.

Row 16: K15, SSK, K5, K2tog, K15. (37 sts)

Row 17: Purl.

Row 18: Cast off 15 sts, SSK, K3, K2tog, K to end. (20 sts)

Row 19: Cast off 15 sts pw, P to end. (5 sts)

Row 20: SSK, K1, K2tog. (3 sts)

Row 21: K1, P1, K1.

Row 22: Knit.

Rows 23–29: Rpt last 2 rows, 3 more times, then rpt row 21 once more.

Row 30: K1, sl1 pw with yarn at back, K1.

Row 31: K1, sl1 pw with yarn at front, K1.

Cast off.

Shoe straps

(make 2)

Using Yarn C and 2.5mm needles cast on 10 sts.

Row 1 (ws): K7, P3.

Row 2: K3, turn.

Row 3: P3.

Cast off knitwise.

Pinafore Dress

Front

Using Yarn C and 3mm needles cast on 37 sts.

Row 1 (ws): Knit.

Rows 2–3: Starting with a knit row, stocking stitch 2 rows.

Row 4: [K4, P2] to last st, K1.

Rows 5–7: Stocking stitch 3 rows.

Row 8: K1, [P2, K4] to end.

Rows 9–11: Stocking stitch 3 rows.

Rows 12–27: Rpt rows 4–11, twice more.

Row 28: [K1, K2tog] to last st, K1. (25 sts)

Row 29: [K1, P1] 3 times, K2, P9, K2, [P1, K1] 3 times.

Row 30: [P1, K1] 3 times, K13, [K1, P1] 3 times.

Rows 31–34: Rpt last 2 rows, 2 more times.

Row 35: Cast off 6 sts in pattern, K2, P9, K2, cast off 6 sts in pattern. (13 sts)

Cut yarn, then rejoin to work on remaining 13 sts.

Row 36: Knit.

Row 37: K2, P9, K2.

Rows 38–45: Rpt last 2 rows, 4 more times.

Rows 46–47: Knit 2 rows.

Cast off.

Back

Using Yarn C and 3mm needles cast on 37 sts.

Row 1 (ws): Knit.

Rows 2–3: Starting with a knit row, stocking stitch 2 rows.

Row 4: [K4, P2] to last st, K1.

Rows 5–7: Stocking stitch 3 rows.

Row 8: K1, [P2, K4] to end.

Rows 9–11: Stocking stitch 3 rows.

Rows 12–27: Rpt rows 4–11, twice more.

Row 28: [K1, K2tog] to last st, K1. (25 sts)

Row 29: [K1, P1] to last st, K1.

Row 30: [P1, K1] to last st, P1.

Rows 31–34: Rpt last 2 rows, 2 more times.

Cast off in pattern.

Dress straps

(make 2)

Using Yarn C and 3mm needles cast on 28 sts.

Row 1 (ws): K25, P3.

Row 2: K3, turn.

Row 3: P3.

Cast off knitwise.

Hoodie

Right front

Using Yarn E and 3mm needles cast on 16 sts.

Row 1 (ws): Knit.

Rows 2–3: Knit 2 rows.

Use Intarsia technique (see Techniques) for changing yarn across the following rows.

(C) = Use Yarn C (D) = Use Yarn D (E) = Use Yarn E

Row 4: (E) K3, (D) K13.

Row 5: (D) P13, (E) K3.

Row 6: (E) K3, (C) K13.

Row 7: (C) P13, (E) K3.

Rows 8–33: Rpt the last 4 rows, 6 more times, then rpt rows 4 & 5 once more.

Cast off.

Left front

Using Yarn E and 3mm needles cast on 16 sts.

Row 1 (ws): Knit.

Rows 2–3: Knit 2 rows.

Use Intarsia technique (see Techniques) for changing yarn across the following rows.

(C) = Use Yarn C (D) = Use Yarn D (E) = Use Yarn E

Row 4: (D) K13, (E) K3.

Row 5: (E) K3, (D) P13.

Row 6: (C) K13, (E) K3.

Row 7: (E) K3, (C) P13.

Rows 8–19: Rpt the last 4 rows, 3 more times.

Row 20: (D) K13, (E) K1, YO, K2tog.

Row 21: (E) K1, Ktbl, K1, (D) P13.

Rows 22–23: Rpt rows 6 & 7.

Rows 24–25: Rpt rows 4 & 5.

Row 26: (C) K13, (E) K1, YO, K2tog.

Row 27: (E) K1, Ktbl, K1, (C) P13.

Rows 28–29: Rpt rows 4 & 5.

Rows 30–31: Rpt rows 6 & 7.

Rows 32–33: Rpt rows 20 & 21.

Cast off.

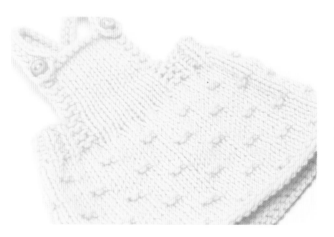

Back

Using Yarn E and 3mm needles cast on 29 sts.

Row 1 (ws): Knit.

Rows 2–3: Knit 2 rows.

Rows 4–33: Starting with a knit row and Yarn D, stocking stitch 30 rows working in a stripe pattern repeat of 2 rows Yarn D and 2 rows Yarn C throughout.

Cast off.

Sleeves

(make 2)

Using Yarn E and 3mm needles cast on 22 sts.

Row 1 (ws): Knit.

Rows 2–3: Knit 2 rows.

Change to Yarn D.

Rows 4–21: Starting with a knit row, stocking stitch 20 rows.

Cast off.

Hood

Using Yarn E and 3mm needles cast on 50 sts.

Row 1 (ws): Knit.

Rows 2–3: Knit 2 rows.

Change to Yarn D.

Rows 4–30: Starting with a knit row and Yarn D, stocking stitch 27 rows working in a stripe pattern repeat of 2 rows Yarn D and 2 rows Yarn C throughout, ending with 1 row of Yarn C.

Cut yarn leaving a long tail, transfer the stitches onto a stitch holder.

Making Up

Doll

See Making Up Your Doll in Techniques. Please note, before joining the top edges of the head together position a small bow on the front of the hair and sew in place (see **A** for position).

Hair bob

1. Transfer all the stitches of the hair bob onto a dpn. Using Kitchener stitch (see Techniques) and the cast off tail, attach the hair piece to the bottom of the head working around the first row of hair stitches, from right to left, as follows:

2. Insert the tapestry needle through the back of the hair 'V' stitch on the head and pull the yarn through **(B)**

3. Next insert the tapestry needle knitwise through the first stitch on the dpn, slipping it off the dpn as you do so **(C)**.

4. Insert the tapestry needle purlwise through the next stitch on the dpn, but do not slip off **(D)**.

5. Repeat steps 2 to 4 until all stitches have been worked.

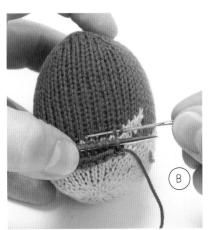

Clothing

Pinafore dress

1. Block all the pieces of the pinafore before making up (see Techniques).

2. Start by sewing up the edge seams matching the pattern up.

3. Sew the straps on to the back edge of the pinafore, around 2cm (¾in) either side of the centre back **(E)**. Crossing the straps over each other first, sew the other end of the straps to the top corners of the bib and then sew on the buttons.

Hoodie

1. Block all the pieces of the Hoodie before making up.

2. Using Mattress stitch (see Techniques) and starting at the outside edges, sew the front and back pieces together at the shoulders, creating a 2cm (¾in) wide shoulder seam at both sides.

3. Transfer the first 25 stitches of the hood onto a dpn and the next 25 stitches onto a second dpn. Join these stitches together using Kitchener stitch (see tip below) to create an invisible seam for the back of the hood.

4. Next sew the bottom edge of the hood around the neck opening, lining up the invisible back seem of the hood to the centre back and the contrast edging of the hood with the button bands at the front.

5. Sew the sleeves to the front and back pieces, lining up the centre of the sleeves to the shoulder seams.

6. Sew up the sleeve and body edge seams to finish.

7. Sew the buttons into place on the right button band, matching them up with the button holes.

Tip

IF YOU ARE UNFAMILIAR WITH KITCHENER STITCH SEE 'JOINING THE TOP EDGES OF THE HEAD USING KITCHENER STITCH' IN TECHNIQUES.

Florence

Florence is very good at maths. This is important because when she set her heart on a rabbit ornament, she was able to work out exactly how long it would take to save up enough pocket money to buy it. Now she's at the shops in her smartest outfit – a knitted skirt and rosy sweater – and the bunny is hers!

You Will Need

Yarn

- **Yarn A** Cream
- **Yarn B** Auburn
- **Yarn C** Pale Pink
- **Yarn D** Cerise
- **Yarn E** Moss Green
- Scraps of black and red for eyes and mouth

Finished size

- 28cm (11in) tall

You will also need

- 3mm (US 2½) straight needles
- 2.5mm (US 1½) straight needles
- 2.5mm (US 1½) double-pointed needles
- Stitch holder
- Tapestry needle
- 3 x 15mm (½in) circles of white felt
- Toy stuffing
- 5 x 6mm (¼in) buttons

Pattern

Cast on using the Long tail cast-on (double cast-on) method (see Techniques) unless otherwise indicated. Where possible leave long tails when you cast on and cast off and use these for the sewing up.

Head

Starting at neck:

Using Yarn A and 2.5mm needles cast on 13 sts.

Row 1 (ws): Purl.

Row 2: [K1, M1] 12 times, K1. (25 sts)

Row 3: Purl.

Row 4: K3, [K1, M1] 7 times, K4, [K1, M1] 7 times, K4. (39 sts)

Rows 5–7: Stocking stitch 3 rows.

Row 8: K3, [K3, M1] 4 times, K6, [K3, M1] 4 times, K6. (47 sts)

Cut yarn.

Rows 9–31: Using Intarsia technique (see Techniques) and working in stocking stitch work Hair Chart. Start with a purl row (ws) at the bottom left hand corner of chart, read purl rows (ws) from left to right and knit rows (rs) from right to left.

For top of head continue in Yarn B.

Row 32: K8, K2tog, K4, SSK, K15, K2tog, K4, SSK, K8. (43 sts)

Row 33: Purl.

Row 34: K8, K2tog, K2, SSK, K15, K2tog, K2, SSK, K8. (39 sts)

Row 35: Purl.

Row 36: K8, K2tog, SSK, K15, K2tog, SSK, K8. (35 sts)

Cut yarn, transfer the stitches onto a stitch holder.

Hair slide
Flower

Using Yarn C and 2.5mm needles cast on 20 sts.

Row 1 (ws): *P1, sl2 pw, pass 1st slip st over 2nd, transfer remaining slip st back onto LH needle and purl, P1; rpt from * to end. (15 sts)

Change to Yarn D.

Row 2: K1, K2 tog to end. (8 sts)

Cast off purlwise.

Cut yarn leaving a long tail, thread tail through the cast off stitches and draw up.

Leaf

Using Yarn E and 2.5mm needles cast on 5 sts.

Row 1 (ws): P3, P1 then slip this stitch back onto LH needle, turn.

Row 2: Pass 1st stitch on RH needle over the 2nd, knit and cast off remaining sts.

Body

Using Yarn A and 2.5mm needles cast on 9 sts.

Starting at neck:

Row 1 (ws): Purl.

Row 2: K1, [K1, M1] 6 times, K2. (15 sts)

Row 3: Purl.

Row 4: K2, [K1, M1] 3 times, K4, [K1, M1] 3 times, K3. (21 sts)

Row 5: Purl.

Row 6: K3, [K1, M1] 4 times, K6, [K1, M1] 4 times, K4. (29 sts)

Rows 7–9: Stocking stitch 3 rows.

Row 10: K4, [K1, M1] 6 times, K8, [K1, M1] 6 times, K5. (41 sts)

Rows 11–15: Stocking stitch 5 rows.

Row 16: K3, [K3, M1] 4 times, K8, [K3, M1] 4 times, K6. (49 sts)

Rows 17–27: Stocking stitch 11 rows.

KNICKERS

Continue working the 49 sts on needle.

Change to Yarn D.

Rows 28–29: Knit 2 rows.

Rows 30–43: Using Fair Isle technique (see Techniques) and working in stocking stitch, work Knicker Chart across the stitches, repeating the stitches within the red border 11 times.

Cast off.

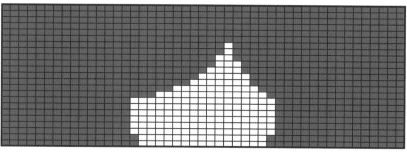

Hair Chart

□ = Yarn A
■ = Yarn B

Arms

(make 2)

Using Yarn A and 2.5mm needles cast on 12 sts.

Rows 1–3: Starting with a purl row (ws), stocking stitch 3 rows.

Row 4: Cast on 3 sts using Knit Cast-on method (see Techniques), knit to end. (15 sts)

Row 5: Cast on 3 sts using Purl Cast-on method (see Techniques), purl to end. (18 sts)

Rows 6–7: Stocking stitch 2 rows.

Row 8: SSK, K14, K2tog. (16 sts)

Row 9: Purl.

Row 10: SSK, K12, K2tog. (14 sts)

Row 11: Purl.

Row 12: SSK, K10, K2tog. (12 sts)

Rows 13–47: Stocking stitch 35 rows.

Row 48: SSK, K8, K2tog. (10 sts)

Row 49: Purl.

Row 50: SSK, K6, K2tog. (8 sts)

Row 51: Purl.

Row 52: SSK, K4, K2tog. (6 sts)

Row 53: Purl.

Row 54: SSK, K2, K2tog. (4 sts)

Row 55: Purl.

Cast off.

Legs

(make 2)

Starting at top of leg:

Using Yarn A and 2.5mm needles cast on 16 sts.

Rows 1–43: Starting with a purl row (ws), stocking stitch 43 rows.

SOCKS

Change to Yarn C.

Rows 44–55: Stocking stitch 12 rows.

TOP OF FOOT

Row 56: Cast off 5 sts, knit to end. (11 sts)

Row 57: Cast off 5 sts pw, purl to end. (6 sts)

Rows 58–75: Stocking stitch 18 rows.

Cast off row: SSK, K2, K2tog (cast off all sts as you work them).

Sock frills

(make 2)

Using Yarn C and 2.5mm needles cast on 17 sts.

Row 1 (ws): [P1, Pfb] to last st, P1. (25 sts)

Row 2: Knit.

Row 3: Purl.

Row 4: Cast off 1 st, *slip remaining stitch back onto LH needle, then cast on 1 st using Knit Cast-on method (see Techniques), cast off 3 sts*; rpt from *to end.

Mary Jane shoes

(make 2)

Using Yarn D and 2.5mm needles cast on 12 sts.

Row 1 (ws): Purl.

Row 2: K1, M1, K3, [K1, M1] 3 times, K4, M1, K1. (17 sts)

Row 3: Purl.

Row 4: [K1, M1] 2 times, K3, [K1, M1] 2 times, K2, [K1, M1] 2 times, K3, [K1, M1] 2 times, K1. (25 sts)

Row 5: Purl.

Row 6: [K2, M1] 2 times, K2, [K2, M1] 2 times, K3, [K2, M1] 2 times, K2, [K2, M1] 2 times, K2. (33 sts)

Row 7: Purl.

Row 8: [K3, M1] 2 times, K1, [K3, M1] 2 times, K4, [K3, M1] 2 times, K1, [K3, M1] 2 times, K3. (41 sts)

Rows 9–13: Stocking stitch 5 rows.

Row 14: K15, SSK, K7, K2tog, K15. (39 sts)

Row 15: Purl.

Row 16: K15, SSK, K5, K2tog, K15. (37 sts)

Row 17: Purl.

Cast off row: K15, SSK, K3, K2tog, K15 (cast off all stitches as you work them).

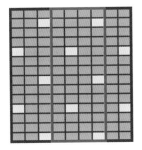

Knicker Chart

▪ = Yarn D

▫ = Yarn C

☐ = Repeat

Shoe straps

(make 2)

Using Yarn D and 2.5mm needles cast on 10 sts.

Row 1 (ws): K7, P3.

Row 2: K3, turn.

Row 3: P3.

Cast off knitwise.

Skirt

Using Yarn E and 3mm needles cast on 66 sts.

Row 1 (ws): Knit.

Row 2: [YO, K2, slip YO over K2] to end.

Row 3: Purl.

Rows 4–21: Rpt last 2 rows, 9 more times.

Row 22: [K2tog, K1] to end. (44 sts)

Rows 23–27: Stocking stitch 5 rows. Change to Yarn D.

Row 28: [K5, sl1 pw, K5] to end.

Row 29: [K5, sl1 pw wyif, K5] to end. Change to Yarn E.

Row 30: Knit.

Row 31: Purl.

Cast off.

Sweater
Front of sweater

Using Yarn C and 3mm needles cast on 27 sts.

Row 1 (ws): Knit.

Rows 2–3: Knit 2 rows.

Rows 4–11: Starting with a knit row, stocking stitch 8 rows.

The Sweater Chart is placed in the following rows using Intarsia technique (see Techniques) and worked in stocking stitch. Starting at the bottom right hand corner, read knit rows (rs) from right to left and purl rows (ws) from left to right.

Row 12: K6, work Sweater Chart, K5.

Row 13: P5, work Sweater Chart, P6.

Rows 14–26: Rpt the last 2 rows 6 more times, then rpt row 12 once more.

Rows 27–33: Stocking stitch 7 rows. Cast off.

Back of sweater

Using Yarn C and 2.5mm needles cast on 27 sts.

Row 1 (ws): Knit.

Rows 2–3: Knit 2 rows.

Rows 4–19: Starting with a knit row, stocking stitch 16 rows.

RIGHT BUTTON PLACKET

Row 20: K15, turn (15 sts).

Row 21: K3, P12.

Rows 22–23: Rpt last 2 rows.

Row 24: K13, YO, K2tog, turn.

Row 25: K1, Ktbl, K1, P12.

Rows 26–31: Rpt rows 20 and 21, 3 more times.

Row 32: Rpt row 24.

Row 33: Rpt row 25.

Cast off 15 sts, cut yarn.

LEFT BUTTON PLACKET

Row 1: Returning to stitches still on needle, rejoin Yarn C and pick up and knit 3 sts from BEHIND the first row of right button placket (see Techniques, Picking Up Stitches), knit across stitches on left hand needle. (15 sts)

Row 2: P12, K3.

Row 3: Knit.

Rows 4–13: Rpt last 2 rows, 5 more times.

Row 14: P12, K3.

Cast off.

Sleeves of sweater

(make 2)

Using Yarn C and 3mm needles cast on 20 sts.

Row 1 (ws): Knit.

Rows 2–17: Starting with a knit row, stocking stitch 16 rows.

Cast off.

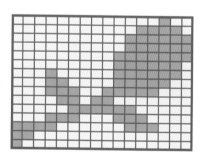

Sweater Chart

☐ = Yarn C

▣ = Yarn D

▪ = Yarn E

Making up

Doll

See Making Up Your Doll in Techniques. Please note, attach the sock frills before sewing the legs to the body, and sew hair slide in place before joining the top edges of the head together.

SOCK FRILLS

Sew frill in place on completed leg. Place tapestry needle through the back of the 'V' stitch on the first row of cream (A), then down through the cast on stitch of the frill (B) and back up through the next cast on stitch (C). Continue in this manner all the way around the sock, making sure both edges of the frill meet at the back. Sew up the back seam of the frill.

(A)

(B)

(C)

Hair slide

1. Secure the leaf to the back of the flower with a couple of stitches.

2. Do not weave in or tie off any of the loose ends yet. As the flower is quite small it is best to push any loose ends through to the inside of the head before sewing in place.

3. Position hair slide on Florence's head and sew in place, stitching through the back loops on the first row of Yarn D and then through the back of the hair stitches **(D)**.

Clothing

Sweater

1. Block all the pieces of the sweater before making up.

2. Start by sewing the buttons into place on the back of the sweater, matching them up with the button holes **(E)**.

3. Sew up shoulder seams leaving a big enough gap to fit around Florence's neck. Sew sleeves to front and back pieces lining up centre of sleeves to shoulder seams. Sew up sleeve and sweater edge seams.

Skirt

1. Block skirt before sewing it up.

2. Starting at the hem sew the edges of the skirt together, creating a centre back seam.

3. Sew button onto the centre front of belt **(F)**.

Martha

When she grows up Martha is going to be a teacher. She's had lots of practice writing on a chalkboard, adding up sums and putting gold stars on her finished work. She reckons jeans and a bright tunic with matching red shoes are the perfect cheerful but practical outfit for a primary school teacher. She can't wait to get into the classroom!

You Will Need

Yarn

- **Yarn A** Mocha
- **Yarn B** Chocolate
- **Yarn C** Bright Red
- **Yarn D** White
- **Yarn E** Denim Blue
- **Yarn F** Sky Blue
- Scraps of black and red for eyes and mouth

Finished size

- 28cm (11in) tall

You will also need

- 3mm (US 2½) straight needles
- 2.5mm (US 1½) straight needles
- 2.5mm (US 1½) double-pointed needles
- Stitch holder
- Stitch markers
- Tapestry needle
- 3 x 15mm (½in) circles of white felt
- Toy stuffing
- 7 x 6mm (¼in) buttons
- 2 short lengths of 5mm wide ribbon

Pattern

Cast on using the Long-tail (double cast on) method (see Techniques) unless otherwise indicated. Where possible leave long tails when you cast on and cast off and use these for the sewing up.

Head

Starting at neck:

Using Yarn A and 2.5mm needles cast on 13 sts.

Row 1 (ws): Purl.

Row 2: [K1, M1] 12 times, K1. (25 sts)

Row 3: Purl.

Row 4: K3, [K1, M1] 7 times, K4, [K1, M1] 7 times, K4. (39 sts)

Rows 5–7: Stocking stitch 3 rows.

Row 8: K3, [K3, M1] 4 times, K6, [K3, M1] 4 times, K6. (47 sts)

Cut yarn.

Rows 9–31: Using Intarsia technique (see Techniques) and working in stocking stitch work Hair Chart. Start with a purl row (ws) at the bottom left hand corner of chart, read purl rows (ws) from left to right and knit rows (rs) from right to left.

For top of head continue in Yarn B.

Row 32: K8, K2tog, K4, SSK, K15, K2tog, K4, SSK, K8. (43 sts)

Row 33: Purl.

Row 34: K8, K2tog, K2, SSK, K15, K2tog, K2, SSK, K8. (39 sts)

Row 35: Purl.

Row 36: K8, K2tog, SSK, K15, K2tog, SSK, K8. (35 sts)

Cut yarn, transfer the stitches onto a stitch holder.

Buns

(make 2)

Using Yarn B and 2.5mm needles cast on 4 sts.

Row 1 (ws): Purl.

Row 2: Kfb to end. (8 sts)

Row 3: Purl.

Row 4: [Kfb] 2 times, K4, [Kfb] 2 times. (12 sts)

Row 5: Purl.

Row 6: Kfb, K10, Kfb. (14 sts)

Rows 7–13: Stocking stitch 7 rows.

Row 14: K2tog, K10, K2tog. (12 sts)

Row 15: Purl.

Row 16: [K2tog] 2 times, K4, [K2tog] 2 times. (8 sts)

Row 17: Purl.

Row 18: K2tog to end. (4 sts)

Cut yarn leaving a long tail, thread tail through the stitches left on needle and draw up.

Body

Using Yarn A and 2.5mm needles cast on 9 sts.

Starting at neck

Row 1 (ws): Purl.

Row 2: K1, [K1, M1] 6 times, K2. (15 sts)

Row 3: Purl.

Row 4: K2, [K1, M1] 3 times, K4, [K1, M1] 3 times, K3. (21 sts)

Row 5: Purl.

Row 6: K3, [K1, M1] 4 times, K6, [K1, M1] 4 times, K4. (29 sts)

Rows 7–9: Stocking stitch 3 rows.

Row 10: K4, [K1, M1] 6 times, K8, [K1, M1] 6 times, K5. (41 sts)

Rows 11–15: Stocking stitch 5 rows.

Row 16: K3, [K3, M1] 4 times, K8, [K3, M1] 4 times, K6. (49 sts)

Rows 17–27: Stocking stitch 11 rows.

KNICKERS

Continue working the 49 sts on needle.

Starting with Yarn D, the knickers are worked in a stripe pattern of 2 rows Yarn D and 2 rows Yarn F throughout.

Rows 28–29: Knit 2 rows.

Rows 30–43: Starting with a knit row, stocking stitch 14 rows.

Cast off using Yarn D.

Arms

(make 2)

Using Yarn A and 2.5mm needles cast on 12 sts.

Rows 1–3: Starting with a purl row (ws), stocking stitch 3 rows.

Row 4: Cast on 3 sts using knit cast-on method (see Techniques section), knit to end. (15 sts)

Row 5: Cast on 3 sts using purl cast-on method (see Techniques section), purl to end. (18 sts)

Rows 6–7: Stocking stitch 2 rows.

Row 8: SSK, K14, K2tog. (16 sts)

Row 9: Purl.

Row 10: SSK, K12, K2tog. (14 sts)

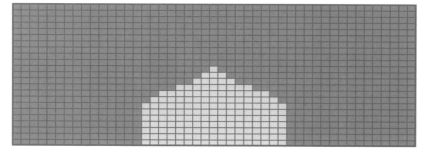

Hair Chart

☐ = Yarn A   ■ = Yarn B

Row 11: Purl.

Row 12: SSK, K10, K2tog. (12 sts)

Rows 13–47: Stocking stitch 35 rows.

Row 48: SSK, K8, K2tog. (10 sts)

Row 49: Purl.

Row 50: SSK, K6, K2tog. (8 sts)

Row 51: Purl.

Row 52: SSK, K4, K2tog. (6 sts)

Row 53: Purl.

Row 54: SSK, K2, K2tog. (4 sts)

Row 55: Purl.

Cast off.

Legs

(make 2)

Starting at top of leg:

Using Yarn A and 2.5mm needles cast on 16 sts.

Rows 1–55: Starting with a purl row (ws), stocking stitch 55 rows.

Row 56: Cast off 5 sts, knit to end. (11 sts)

Row 57: Cast off 5 sts pw, purl to end. (6 sts)

TOP OF FOOT

Rows 58–75: Stocking stitch 18 rows.

Cast off row: SSK, K2, K2tog (cast off all sts as you work them).

Mary Jane Shoes

(make 2)

Using Yarn C and 2.5mm needles cast on 12 sts.

Row 1 (ws): Purl.

Row 2: K1, M1, K3, [K1, M1] 3 times, K4, M1, K1. (17 sts)

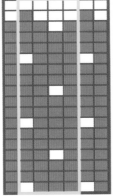

Row 3: Purl.

Row 4: [K1, M1] 2 times, K3, [K1, M1] 2 times, K2, [K1, M1] 2 times, K3, [K1, M1] 2 times, K1. (25 sts)

Row 5: Purl.

Row 6: [K2, M1] 2 times, K2, [K2, M1] 2 times, K3, [K2, M1] 2 times, K2, [K2, M1] 2 times, K2. (33 sts)

Row 7: Purl.

Row 8: [K3, M1] 2 times, K1, [K3, M1] 2 times, K4, [K3, M1] 2 times, K1, [K3, M1] 2 times, K3. (41 sts)

Rows 9–13: Stocking stitch 5 rows.

Row 14: K15, SSK, K7, K2tog, K15. (39 sts)

Row 15: Purl.

Row 16: K15, SSK, K5, K2tog, K15. (37 sts)

Row 17: Purl.

Cast off row: K15, SSK, K3, K2tog, K15 (cast off all stitches as you work them).

Shoe straps

(make 2)

Using Yarn C and 2.5mm needles cast on 10 sts.

Row 1 (ws): K7, P3.

Row 2: K3, turn.

Row 3: P3.

Cast off knitwise.

Tunic

The tunic is worked from the top down in one piece and fastened down the back. The button bands (first and last 3 sts on each row) are worked in Yarn C throughout, using Intarsia method

(see Techniques). Colour changes along rows are indicated in brackets.

(C) = Use Yarn C   (D) = Use Yarn D

Using Yarn C and 3mm needles cast on 23 sts.

Row 1 (ws): K6, pm, K2, pm, K8, pm, K2, pm, K5.

Row 2: K1, YO, K2tog, [K to marker, m1r, sm, K1, m1l] 4 times, K to end. (31 sts)

Row 3: (C) K3, (D) purl to last 3 sts, (C) K1, Ktbl, K1.

Row 4: (C) K3, (D) [K to marker, m1r, sm, K1, m1l] 4 times, K to last 3 sts, (C) K3. (39 sts)

Row 5: K3, purl to last 3 sts, K3.

Row 6: [K to marker, m1r, sm, K1, m1l] 4 times, K to end. (47 sts)

Row 7: Rpt row 3.

Row 8: Rpt row 4. (55 sts)

Row 9: Rpt row 5.

Row 10: Rpt row 2. (63 sts)

Row 11: Rpt row 3.

Row 12: Rpt row 4. (71 sts)

Row 13: Rpt row 5.

Row 14: Rpt row 6. (79 sts)

Row 15: Rpt row 3.

Row 16: Rpt row 4. (87 sts)

The stitch markers are no longer needed.

Row 17: K3, P11, K17, P25, K17, P11, K3.

Row 18: K1, YO, K2tog, K11, cast off 17 sts, K25, cast off 17 sts, K to end. (53 sts)

Row 19: K3, Pfb, [P2, Pfb] 3 times, [Pfb] twice, [Pfb, P2] 7 times, Pfb, P1, [Pfb] twice, [Pfb, P2] 3 times, Pfb, K1, Ktbl, K1. (73 sts)

Tunic Chart is worked over rows 20–37. Using Fair Isle technique (see Techniques) and working in stocking stitch, work Tunic Chart across the middle 67 stitches of each row, repeating the stitches within the yellow border 16 times.

Row 20: K3, work Tunic Chart, K3.

Rows 21–25: Rpt last row, 5 more times.

Tunic Chart

- ■ = Yarn C
- □ = Yarn D
- ▢ = Repeat

Row 26: K1, YO, K2tog, work Tunic Chart, K3.

Row 27: K3, work Tunic Chart, K1, Ktbl, K1.

Row 28: K3, work Tunic Chart, K3.

Rows 29–33: Rpt last row, 5 more times.

Row 34: K1, YO, K2tog, work Tunic Chart, K3.

Row 35: K3, work Tunic Chart, K1, Ktbl, K1.

Row 36: K3, work Tunic Chart, K3.

Row 37: K3, work Tunic Chart, K3.

Rows 38–41: Knit 4 rows.

Cast off.

Jeans

Made in one piece and seamed at the inside leg and back of body.

Left leg

Starting at the bottom of left leg:

Using Yarn F and 3mm needles cast on 25 sts.

Row 1 (ws): Purl.

Row 2: Knit.

Row 3: P1, P2tog, P10, P2tog, P to end. (23 sts)

Change to Yarn E.

Rows 4–41: Stocking stitch 38 rows.

Row 42: Kfb, K to last st, Kfb. (25 sts)

Slip all stitches onto a stitch holder.

Cut yarn leaving a small tail to weave in later.

Right leg

Work rows 1–42 as left leg.

Row 43: Purl.

Leave these stitches on the right hand needle and do not cut the yarn

JOIN LEGS

Slip the stitches from the stitch holder back onto the left-hand knitting needle, purl to the end of the row. You should now have 50 sts on the needle.

Rows 44–57: Stocking stitch 14 rows.

Change to Yarn C.

Row 58: *K1, [K3, sl1, K4] 3 times*; rpt from *to*.

Row 59: *[K4, sl1 wyif, K3] 3 times, K1*; rpt from *to*.

Change to Yarn E.

Rows 60–61: Starting with a knit row, stocking stitch 2 rows.

Cast off.

Making Up

Doll

See Making Up Your Doll in Techniques.

Buns

1. Sew a running stitch with yarn tail (shown in red in the photographs for clarity – yours should be brown) around the edge and pull tightly, stuffing firmly as you go and then knot both tail ends together tightly to secure (**A, B and C**).

2. Sew buns in position at each side of head then finish with a small piece of ribbon tied in a bow (**D**).

Clothing

Tunic

Block the tunic then sew the buttons into place on the back of the tunic, matching them up with the button holes (**E**).

Jeans

1. Block the jeans before making up.

2. Sew up the inside leg seams to crotch, followed by the back seam.

TECHNIQUES

MAKING UP YOUR DOLL

The dolls all share some features and common techniques in their assembly. In this section you'll find everything you need to know about completing your doll's head, body, arms and legs. Please read the individual making up notes in each pattern first before following the instructions in this section. For all dolls bear the following in mind when assembling their parts.

· Where possible use the cast on/cast off tails for sewing up. Tie off or weave in any other loose ends as you go.

· Use a tapestry needle and mattress stitch (unless otherwise indicated) for sewing up seams.

· Use a sewing needle and thread to attach buttons.

BODY

1. Starting at the bottom, sew up the back edges of the body, making sure to match up colour changes.

2. Leave an opening at the neck big enough to push the stuffing through, of about 2.5cm (1in). With the back seam central to the doll's back, sew together the bottom edges of body, stitching through the outside loops of the cast off stitches **(A and B)**.

3. Stuff firmly and close up neck seam, then bury loose ends inside body.

LEGS

Each doll has a particular style of footwear – either May Jane shoes, T-bar shoes, Sneakers or Boots. Please follow the making up instructions that correspond with the feet of your doll.

Legs with Mary Jane shoes
Right leg and shoe

1. Sew the top of shoe to the base of the leg and around the foot, using mattress stitch on the leg and foot but only sew through the second row of back loops on the shoe **(C, D, E and F)**. Make sure the end of the foot is centered between the decreases at the front of the shoe.

2. Sew the strap onto the left edge of the shoe, pull the ends through to inside and secure.

3. Stitch a button on the opposite end of strap, and secure it to the shoe.

4. Sew bottom edges of shoe together, working from the toe end towards the ankle. Stuff the foot firmly.

5. Sew the leg edges together, making sure any colour changes line up, stuffing as you go. Only lightly stuff the top part of the legs to enable them to move into a sitting position.

Left Leg & Shoe

Make up in the same way as the right leg and shoe, but sew the strap onto the right edge of the shoe instead of the left.

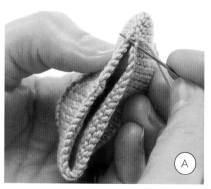

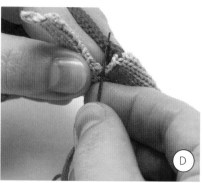

Legs with T-bar shoes
Right Leg and shoe

1. Begin by sewing the top of the shoe to the base of the leg and around the foot in the same way as the Mary Jane shoes continuing along the same row of back loops as you go around the toe of the shoe (see dotted line in **G** for position).

2. Insert the shoe strap through the loop formed by the slipped stitches at the top of the T-bar, you may need to thread the cast on and off tails on to a tapestry needle first and use these to pull it through (**H and I**). Sew end of shoe strap onto left edge of shoe, pull ends through to inside and secure.

3. Stitch a button onto the opposite end of the strap, and secure it to the shoe.

4. Sew the bottom edges of the shoe together, starting at the toe working through to the ankle. Then stuff the foot firmly. If necessary adjust vertical T-bar strap so that it lies in the centre of the foot .

5. Sew the leg edges together, making sure any colour changes line up, stuffing as you go. Only lightly stuff the top part of the legs to enable them to move into a sitting position.

Left leg and shoe

Make up in the same way as the right leg and shoe, but sew the strap onto the right edge of the shoe instead of the left.

Legs with boots

1. Using whip stitch (see Casting On and Stitches), sew together the 'cast off' edges at top of foot (**J**).

2. Sew the bottom edges of the boot together, starting at the toe working through to the ankle.

3. Then stuff the foot firmly.

4. Sew the leg edges together, making sure colour changes line up, stuffing as you go. Only lightly stuff the top part of the legs to enable them to move into a sitting position.

Boot cuffs

1. Sew side edges together using mattress stitch.

2. Turn the cuff inside out and slide into position over the leg, line up the seam on the cuff with the seam on the back of the leg. Stitch it into place by sewing the cast-off edge of the cuff to the leg at the ankle, on the last row of the boot stitches (**K**).

3. Fold over the top of the cuffs to finish the boots (**L**).

(G)

(H)

(I)

(J)

(K)

(L)

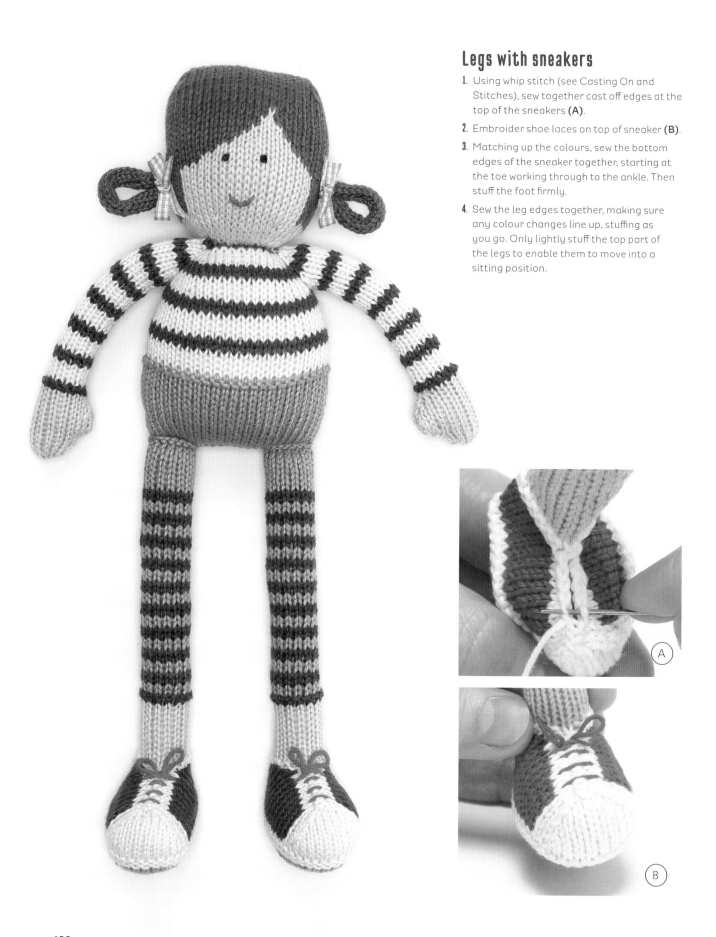

Legs with sneakers

1. Using whip stitch (see Casting On and Stitches), sew together cast off edges at the top of the sneakers **(A)**.

2. Embroider shoe laces on top of sneaker **(B)**.

3. Matching up the colours, sew the bottom edges of the sneaker together, starting at the toe working through to the ankle. Then stuff the foot firmly.

4. Sew the leg edges together, making sure any colour changes line up, stuffing as you go. Only lightly stuff the top part of the legs to enable them to move into a sitting position.

Sewing the legs to the body

1. Insert the tapestry needle through the back of the 'V' stitch on the first row of the body **(C)**, then down through the cast on stitch of the leg **(D)** and back up through the next cast on stitch **(E)**. Continue in this manner all the way around the leg, but go through the back of two 'V' stitches together at the outer corner of the body seam **(F)**.

ARMS

1. Using a tapestry needle thread the yarn through the cast on stitches at the start of the hand and draw up **(G and H)**.
2. Sew the side edges together, stuffing the hand and arm firmly as you go, leaving the tapered top of the arm open.
3. Sew the tapered edges of the arm to the body, stuffing lightly as you go (see **I** for position).

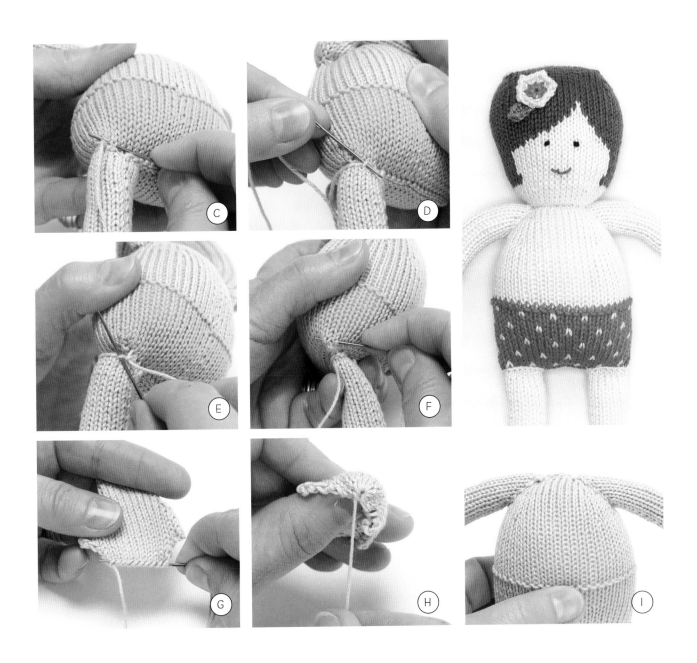

Blocking

Blocking your work will help create a flat, neat finish and help stop edges from curling. Use rust proof pins and leave to dry completely before removing pins. You can use spray blocking or steam blocking with cotton yarn.

Spray blocking

Spray the knitted piece with cold water until it is damp but not saturated. Pin flat, and leave to dry completely.

Steam blocking

Pin the knitted piece flat and hold a steam iron close to the fabric and steam until it is damp (do not touch the fabric with the iron). Leave to dry.

HEAD
Adding the face detail

Take a small circle of white felt and place at the back of the work behind where you plan to embroider the first eye. Using the black yarn place a couple of small stitches to form the eye and knot the black thread securely at the back of the work, trim off the excess. Repeat for the second eye. Embroider mouth in the same way as eyes **(A and B)**.

Joining the top edges of the head using Kitchener stitch

At the making up phase of each doll, the top stitches of the head are joined as follows:

Transfer first 9 stitches onto a double pointed needle, middle 17 stitches onto second double pointed needle and last 9 stitches onto opposite end of first double pointed needle **(C and D)**.

Next, join the top edges using Kitchener stitch (grafting) as follows:
1. Thread a tapestry needle with a length of Yarn E. Hold the work with the stitches parallel in your left hand. Insert the tapestry needle through the first stitch on the front needle as if to PURL **(E)**. Pull the yarn through, leaving a tail that you will weave in later. Leave the stitch on the front needle.

2. Insert the tapestry needle through the first stitch on the back needle as if to KNIT **(F)**, pull the yarn through, leaving the stitch on the back needle.

3. Insert the tapestry needle through the first stitch on the front needle as if to KNIT, pull the yarn through, removing the stitch from the front needle. Insert the tapestry needle through the next stitch on the front needle as if to PURL, pull the yarn through, leaving the stitch on the front needle.

4. Insert the tapestry needle through the first stitch on the back needle as if to PURL, pull the yarn through, removing the stitch from the back needle. Insert the tapestry needle through the next stitch on the back needle as if to KNIT, pull the yarn through, leaving the stitch on the back needle.

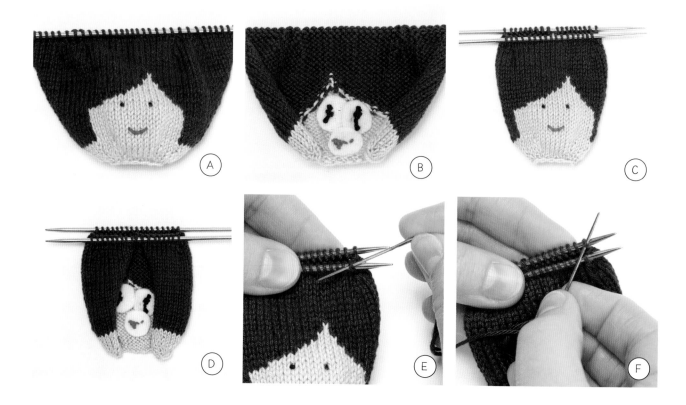

Repeat step 3 and step 4 until you have 11sts left on the back needle and 9 sts left on the front needle.

5. Insert the tapestry needle through the next stitch on the back needle as if to PURL, pull the yarn through, removing the stitch from the back needle. Insert the tapestry needle through the next two stitches together on the back needle as if to KNIT **(G)**, pull the yarn through, leaving these two stitches on the back needle.

Repeat step 3.

6. Insert the tapestry needle through the first two stitches together on the back needle as if to PURL, pull the yarn through, removing the two stitches from the back needle **(H)**. Insert the tapestry needle through the next stitch on the back needle as if to KNIT, pull the yarn through, leaving the stitch on the back needle.

Repeat step 3 and step 4 until all the stitches have been worked.

Sewing up the head

Starting at the top, join the back edges of the head together, leaving a big enough gap at the neck to push the stuffing through. Stuff and close up the gap, drawing up the ends.

Once the head is complete, sew to the top of the body (see dotted line in figure **(I)** for position).

Making up plaits

1. Wrap yarn around a small piece of card (roughly 9cm (3½in) wide for longer plaits and 6.5cm (2½in) wide for shorter plaits) 12 times **(J)**.

2. Thread a short length of yarn through the top of the loops and secure tightly. Cut yarn through the bottom of the loops **(K)**.

3. Divide into three equal sets of strands and plait.

4. Wrap a short length of yarn around the bottom of the plait and secure tightly. Using your tapestry needle, thread the two loose ends back through the middle of the plait **(L)**.

5. Trim uneven ends to neaten up **(M)**.

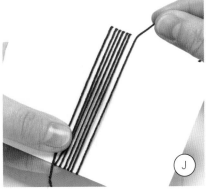

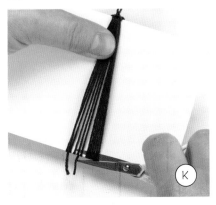

CASTING ON AND STITCHES

Long tail cast-on

(also known as double cast-on)

To make sure you have a long enough tail to cast on your stitches, wrap the yarn around the needle the same amount of times as the amount of stitches you need plus about 25cm (10in) extra to use for sewing up later if needed.

1. Make a slip knot **(A)**.

2. With needle in your right hand, keeping the ball end closest to you, place your left thumb and forefinger between the two strands of yarn. Grasp the loose ends with your other fingers and hold in palm **(B)**.

3. Spread your thumb and forefinger apart to make yarn taught, then move your thumb up towards the tip of the needle, keeping your palm facing forwards **(C)**.

4. Bring the tip of the needle up through the loop on your thumb **(D)**.

5. Then over the top and around the yarn on your forefinger **(E)**.

6. Take the needle back through the thumb loop (insert from top) **(F)**.

7. Gently pull your thumb out and pull on tail ends to tighten the stitch **(G)**.

8. Repeat steps 3–7 **(H)**.

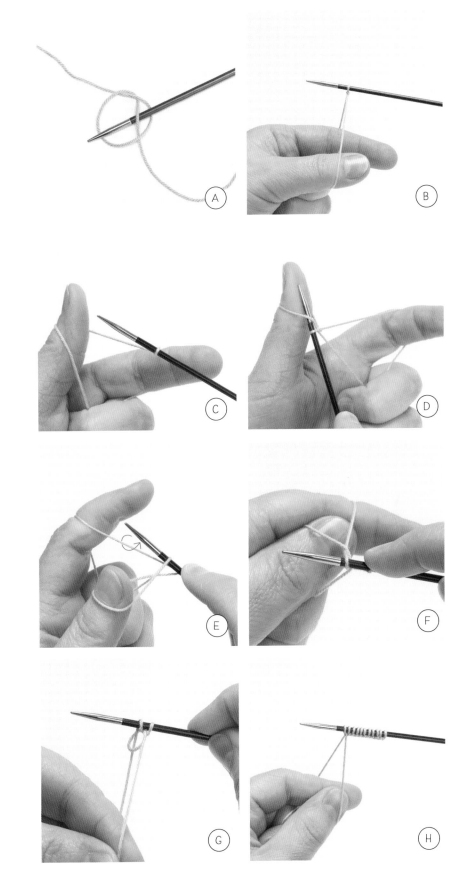

Knit cast-on

1. Insert the right needle into the stitch and knit, but do not take the left-hand stitch off the needle (A).
2. Transfer the loop from the right needle to the left needle (B).
3. Repeat steps 1 and 2 (C).

Purl cast-on

1. Insert the right needle into the stitch and purl, but do not take the left hand stitch off the needle (D).
2. Transfer the loop on the right needle to the left needle (E).
3. Repeat steps 1 and 2 (F).

Picking up stitches

(behind button placket)

1. Working from right to left on the first three stitches of the right button placket **(G)**, insert right needle through the back loop of stitch **(H)**.

2. Wrap yarn around needle and pull through as if to knit **(I)**.

3. Repeat steps 1 and 2 for next two stitches **(J)**.

I-cord

(worked on two double-pointed needles)

1. Cast on number of stitches needed using Long tail cast-on **(K)**.

2. Without turning your work, slide stitches to the right-hand end of needle **(L)**.

3. Bringing the working yarn around the back, knit the first stitch, pulling the yarn tight and knit to the end of the row **(M)**.

4. Repeat steps 2 and 3 until the required length is reached, tugging on the cast-on tail after every row to form into a tube **(N)**.

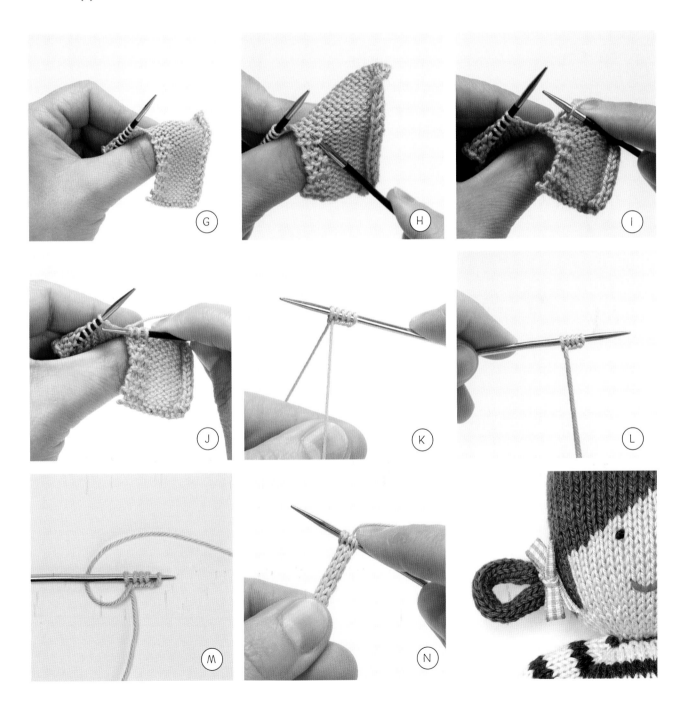

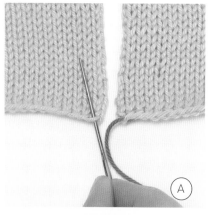

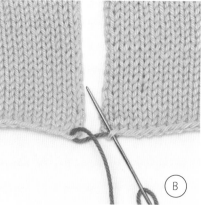

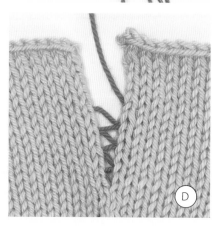

Mattress stitch

Thread the tail (or a length of yarn) onto a tapestry needle. Start with the right sides up and edges side by side.

Vertical mattress stitch

This stitch is used for seaming two selvedge edges together.

1. Insert the needle up through the first cast-on or cast-off loop on the opposite piece, then do the same on the first piece and pull the yarn through **(A and B)**.

2. Take the needle across to the opposite edge again and insert from the front under two horizontal bars in the middle of the outermost stitches **(C)**.

3. Repeat step 2, working back and forth across each side, gently pulling the yarn through to close the seam **(D)**.

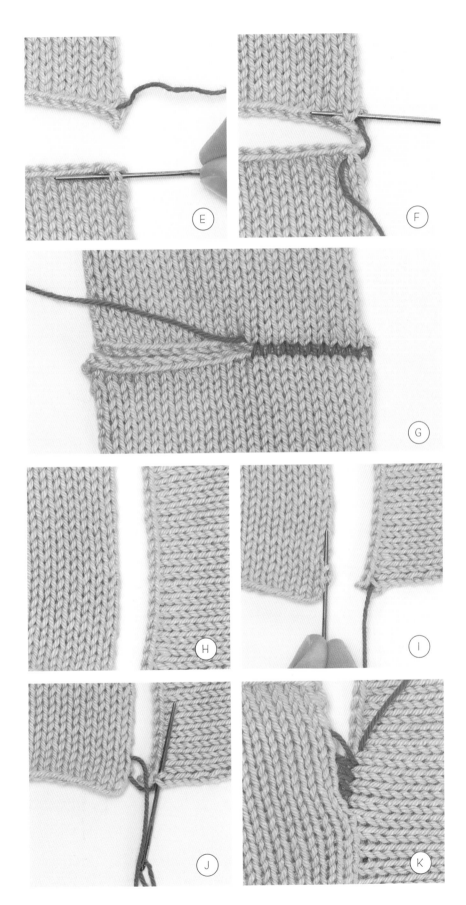

Horizontal mattress stitch

This stitch is used for seaming the cast on or cast off edges together.

1. Insert needle under the 'V' of the first stitch and pull yarn through (**E**).
2. Take the needle across to the other edge and do the same with the stitch on that side (**F**).
3. Repeat steps 1 and 2, working back and forth across each side, gently pulling the yarn through to close the seam (**G**).

Vertical to horizontal mattress stitch

This stitch is used for seaming the cast-on or cast-off edge to a selvedge edge (**H**).

1. Insert your needle from the front under two horizontal bars in the middle of the outermost stitches on the selvedge edge and pull the yarn through (**I**).
2. Take the needle across to the cast-on/off-edge and insert under the 'V' of the first stitch (**J**).
3. Repeat steps 1 and 2, working back and forth across each side, gently pulling the yarn through to close the seam (**K**).

French knot

1. Bring the needle through from the back where you want the French knot to be.

2. Wrap the yarn around the needle twice (E).

3. Holding the yarn taught insert the needle back through the same place and draw the yarn through (F) to create the finished knot (G).

Whip stitch

With edges side by side and working from left to right:

1. Insert a threaded tapestry needle through the outer loops of the first cast-off stitch of both edges, pull yarn through leaving a short tail to weave in (H).

2. Insert needle through outer loop of stitch just worked on right hand edge and next stitch up on opposite edge, pull yarn through (I).

3. Insert needle through outer loop of next stitch on each edge and pull yarn through (J).

4. Repeat step 3 for each remaining cast-off stitch (K).

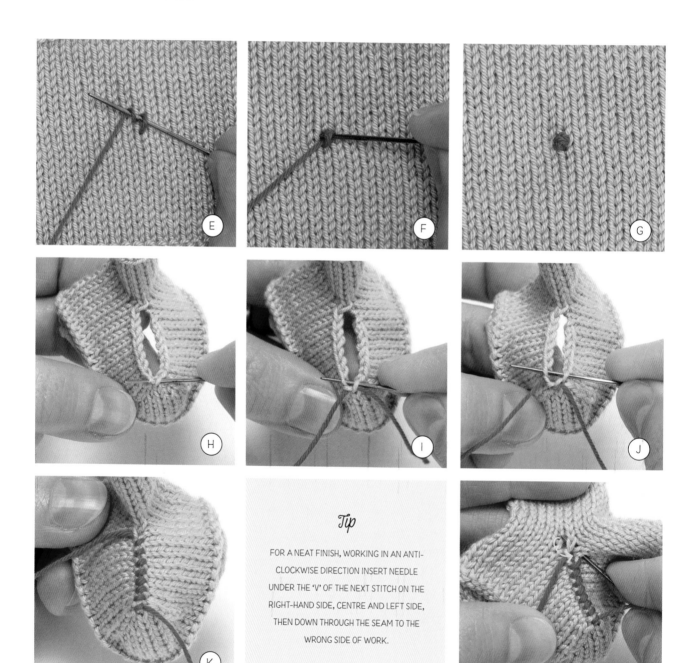

Tip

FOR A NEAT FINISH, WORKING IN AN ANTI-CLOCKWISE DIRECTION INSERT NEEDLE UNDER THE 'V' OF THE NEXT STITCH ON THE RIGHT-HAND SIDE, CENTRE AND LEFT SIDE, THEN DOWN THROUGH THE SEAM TO THE WRONG SIDE OF WORK.

COLOURWORK

All of the dolls in this book use some sort of colour changing techniques. Many of the girls wear striped tights, so if you knit a few dolls you'll become a master of this simple colour change technique. You'll also find instructions on working Fair Isle, Duplicate Stitch and Intarsia, which you will need in order to create the decorated sweaters and dresses in this book. If any of these techniques are new to you don't be afraid, they are all easier than they look!

Stripes

When working stripes, carry the yarn up the side of the work. Simply drop the old colour at the back of the work and pick up the new colour to work the first stitch (**A**).

For thicker stripes (more than four rows) catch the old yarn every couple of rows by twisting it with the working yarn stitch (**B**).

Fair Isle (stranded)

Fair Isle is a technique for working two (or more) colours of yarn in the same row, carrying the yarn at the back of the work. As you change colours simply let the old yarn hang down at the back of the work until needed again and pick up the new yarn to work the next stitch. Try not to pull too tightly when changing colours (**C and D**).

Duplicate stitch

(also known as Swiss darning)

Duplicate stitch is a technique allowing you to add small areas of colour to your completed fabric, duplicating the original stitches.

1. Thread your needle with a long piece of the contrast yarn and bring it up through the bottom of the 'V' of the first stitch to duplicate **(A)**.

2. Take the needle under the stitch above **(B)**.

3. Finally go back through the 'V' point of the stitch again **(C)**.

4. Repeat across the row for each area of colour **(D)**.

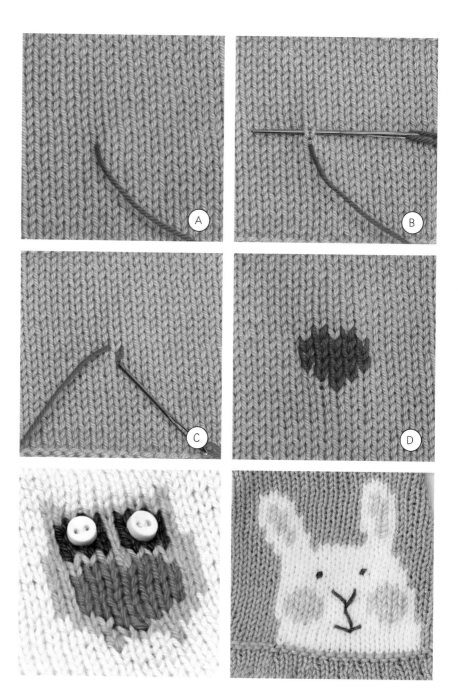

Intarsia

Intarsia uses separate lengths or balls of yarn for each area of colour (as opposed to yarns being carried at the back of the work). Although if there is only one stitch between two areas of the same colour the same length of yarn can be used for both and carried across the back of the single stitch.

It is best to work out how many changes of colour there are before starting and wind the longer lengths of yarn onto separate bobbins or clothes pegs.

For example, to work this sample heart chart you would need three lengths of pink yarn and two lengths of red yarn (each separate length of colour needed is indicated by a different symbol on the chart).

When following a chart, work from the bottom to the top and read purl rows (ws) from left to right and knit rows (rs) from right to left. This sample chart is

worked in stocking stitch and the first row is a purl row, therefore you would begin reading it in the bottom left-hand corner.

An easy way to estimate how much yarn is needed is to count the number of stitches on the chart for each yarn length. Loosely wrap the yarn around your needle once for each stitch then add a further 15cm (6in) for each tail.

To avoid holes between two blocks of colour, work until you need to change colour. Put the needle in the next stitch ready to work it, but pull the old yarn to the left before bringing the new colour yarn up and over it to work the stitch (E).

To tighten up any loose stitches once finished, working on the right side of fabric, insert a tapestry needle into one leg of the loose stitch and pull towards you gently. Repeat on the next few stitches to even out the tension (F).

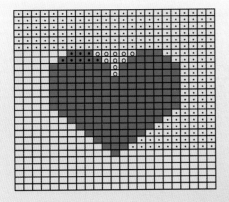

Intarsia Chart

□ = Pink yarn, length 1
⊡ = Pink yarn, length 2
◉ = Pink yarn, length 3
■ = Red yarn, length 1
▣ = Red yarn, length 2

PERSONALISING YOUR DOLL

When it comes to creating a unique personality for your doll, your imagination is the only limitation. Facial expression, hair colour and skin tone, clothing and accessories can all be altered to make the perfect doll for you. Here are just a few ideas to fuel your creativity...

Personalising the hair

Consider changing the hair colour to match the recipient of your doll. It would be fun to create a red-headed version of Jane to give to the auburn-haired little girl in your life.

Why not change the hair style of your doll? You can mix and match any of the hair graphs, pigtail styles and hair embellishments to create your own style. Make pigtails really long, like Pippi Longstocking, or add some ribbon to Polly's plaits.

Personalising the skin and eye colour

You may also want to consider personalising the skin or eye colour of the doll you're making, as well as the hair. There are plenty of different coloured yarns available to represent any skin colour, I have used a few different ones for the dolls throughout this book. Although I have used scraps of black for the eyes on my dolls you could easily substitute scraps of blue, green or brown instead.

Personalising the outfits

Mix and match any of the clothing and accessories and try out new colour combinations to create a whole new wardrobe of outfits for your doll.

ABOUT THE AUTHOR

Louise's love of knitting started when her eldest son came home from school one day saying he wanted to learn how to knit... his interest in knitting lasted about a week, but she has been hooked ever since!

Louise, who has a background in textile design, has developed her own successful brand selling knitting patterns for toys and dolls. Her work has been featured in various craft and knitting magazines, and this is her first book.

To find out more about Louise's work visit her blog at www.boo-biloo.blogspot.co.uk

THANK YOU

Thanks to the publishing team, especially Sarah for giving me this opportunity and making the book possible, Anna for her artistic talents, Jane for helping me out when my brain had stopped working and Lynne for her excellent pattern editing.

Thanks also to Petra for patiently answering my 'what do you think?' questions (of which there were many), and to my friends and family for all your enthusiasm and encouragement.

Thanks to my two sons, Jake and Zachary, for not moaning about all the times my mind has been elsewhere in the last few months.

Finally, special thanks go to my husband Kevin, who as always, has been my tower of strength.

Suppliers

Boo-Biloo
www.etsy.com/uk/shop/BooBiloo
www.ravelry.com/designers/boo-biloo

Deramores
www.deramores.com

LoveCrafts
www.lovecrafts.com

Wool Warehouse
www.woolwarehouse.co.uk

Purple Linda Crafts
www.purplelindacrafts.co.uk

Index

abbreviations 13
Alice Doll 80–7
Anna Doll 58–63
arms 18, 27, 34–5, 40, 46–7, 54, 60, 67, 74, 82, 91, 98–9, 107

bags 78
    flower bag 21, 22
    handles 56, 76, 78
    Scottie dog 76
    shopper bag 56
berets 77, 78
blocking 108
bob hairstyle 85
bobble hat 21, 22
bodies 18, 26, 34, 40, 46, 54, 60, 67, 74, 82, 90, 98, 104, 107
bolero jackets 20–1, 22
boots 47, 54–5, 61, 105
boxer shorts 34, 35
bracelets 27, 30
bun hairstyle 98, 101
bunny hats 49, 50

cardigans 68–9, 70, 76, 78
casting on
    knit cast-on 112
    long-tail cast-on 110–11
    purl cast-on 112
clothing
    bolero jackets 20–1, 22
    boxer shorts 34, 35
    cardigans 68–9, 70, 76, 78
    dresses 19–20, 22, 28–30, 41–2, 47–50, 67–9, 84, 86
    dungarees 35, 36
    hoodies 84–5, 86
    jeans 100
    jeggings 41
    knickers 82, 90, 98
    leggings 74, 75
    personalising 123
    pinafore dress 84, 86
    shorts 56
    shrugs 29, 30
    skirts 61, 62, 75, 77, 92, 94
    socks 35, 83, 91, 93
    sweaters 61–2, 92, 94
    T-shirts 74, 82
    tights 26, 46, 47, 54, 55, 60, 61
    tunics 55, 56, 99–100
colourwork 118–21

dresses 19–20, 22, 28–30, 41–2, 47–50, 67–9
    pinafore dress 84, 86
dungarees 35, 36
duplicate stitch 120

eye colour 123

facial details 108–9, 123
Fair Isle 119
Faye Doll 44–51
felt 12
Florence Doll 88–95
flowers 68
    flower bag 21, 22
    flower hair slides 90
    flower head bands 66
French knot 116
frills 91, 93

Grace Doll 24–31

hair 18, 36, 42, 54, 60, 74
    bobs 85
    buns 98, 101
    personalising 123
    pigtails 26, 30, 46, 60, 62, 66, 69, 77
    plaits 42, 56, 109
hair scrunchies 26, 30
hair slides 90, 94
handles, bag 56, 76, 78
hats 42
    berets 77, 78
    bobble hats 21, 22
    bunny hats 49, 50
head bands 66, 70
heads 18, 26, 34, 40, 46, 54, 60, 66, 74, 82, 90, 98, 108–9
hoodies 84–5, 86

I-cord 113
Intarsia 121

jackets, bolero 20–1, 22
Jane Doll 72–9
jeans 100
jeggings 41

Kitchener stitch 108–9
knickers 82, 90, 98
knit cast-on 112

leaves 90
leggings 74, 75
legs 19, 27, 35, 40–1, 47, 54–6, 61, 67, 75, 83, 91, 99, 104–7
long-tail cast on 110–11

making up 104–9
    Alice Doll 85
    Anna Doll 62
    Faye Doll 50
    Florence Doll 93–4
    Grace Doll 30
    Jane Doll 77–8
    Martha Doll 100
    Naomi Doll 22
    Penny Doll 42
    Pippa Doll 69–70
    Polly Doll 56
    Ralph Doll 36
Martha Doll 96–101
materials 10–12
mattress stitch 114–15
    horizontal 115
    vertical 114
    vertical to horizontal 115

Naomi Doll 16–23
needles 11

Penny Doll 38–43
personalising dolls 122–3
picking up stitches 113
pigtails 26, 30, 46, 60, 62, 66, 69, 77
pinafore dresses 84, 86
Pippa Doll 64–71
plackets 20, 28–9, 41–2, 48–9, 62, 68, 92
plaits 42, 56, 109
pockets 35, 42
Polly Doll 52–7
purl cast-on 112

Ralph Doll 32–7

Scottie dog bag 76
scrunchies 26, 30
shoes
    Mary Jane 19, 91–2, 99, 104
    sneakers 40–1, 75, 106
    straps 19, 28, 67, 83, 92, 99, 104, 105
    T-bar 27–8, 67, 83, 105
    see also boots

shopper bags 56
shorts 56
shrugs 29, 30
skin colour 123
skirts 61, 62, 75, 77, 92, 94
sneakers 35, 40–1, 75, 106
socks 35, 83, 91, 93
spray blocking 108
steam blocking 108
stitches
    duplicate 120
    French knot 116
    horizontal 115
    Kitchener 108–9
    mattress 114–15
    picking up 113
    whip 116
straps
    dress 84
    dungaree 35, 36
    pinafore dress 84, 86
    shoe 19, 28, 67, 83, 92, 99, 104, 105
stripes 119
stuffing 11
sweaters 61–2, 92, 94

T-shirts 74, 82
tights 26, 46, 47, 54, 55, 60, 61
tools 10–12
tunics 55, 56, 99–100

washing 12
whip stitch 116

yarn 11

A DAVID AND CHARLES BOOK
© David and Charles, Ltd 2016

David and Charles is an imprint of David and Charles, Ltd
Suite A, Tourism House, Pynes Hill, Exeter, EX2 5WS

Text and Designs © Louise Crowther 2016
Layout and Photography © David and Charles, Ltd 2016

First published in the UK and USA in 2016

A catalogue record for this book is available from the British Library.

ISBN-13: 9781446306352 paperback
ISBN-13: 9781446374238 EPUB

Printed in Turkey by Omur for:
David and Charles, Ltd
Suite A, Tourism House, Pynes Hill, Exeter, EX2 5WS

20 19 18 17 16 15 14 13 12

Acquisitions Editor: Sarah Callard
Desk Editor: Emma Gardner
Editorial Assistant: Emma Fletcher
Project Editor: Jane Trollope
Art Editor: Anna Wade
Designer: Courtney Kyle
Production Manager: Beverley Richardson
Photography: Jason Jenkins
Art Direction and Styling: Anna Wade

David and Charles publishes high-quality books on a wide range of subjects. For more information visit www.davidandcharles.com.

Layout of the digital edition of this book may vary depending on reader hardware and display settings.